# RICH BROTT

# PROSPERITY

## H A S A

# PURPOSE

## 27 BIBLICAL PRINCIPLES TO UNDERSTAND

I0081232

Published by

# ABC Book Publishing

---

AbcBookPublishing.com
Printed in U.S.A.

**Prosperity Has a Purpose!**
*27 Biblical Principles to Understand*

©Copyright 2008 by Richard A. Brott
10 Digit ISBN: 1-60185-006-9
13 Digit ISBN (EAN): 978-1-60185-006-5

All scripture quotations, unless otherwise indicated, are taken from the *Holy Bible, New International Version*®. *NIV*®. Copyright © 1973, 1978, 1984 by International Bible Society. Used by permission of Zondervan Publishing House. All rights reserved.

Other Versions used are:

*AMP- Amplified Bible.*

*Amer. Std.-American Standard Version*, 1901.

*KJV-King James Version. Authorized King James Version.*

*NASB*-Scripture taken from the *New American Standard Bible*, ©1960, 1962, 1963, 1968, 1971, 1972, 1973, 1975, 1977 by The Lockman Foundation. Used by permission.

Scripture taken from the *New King James Version*. Copyright © 1979, 1980, 1982 by Thomas Nelson, Inc. Publishers. Used by permission. All rights reserved.

Verses marked (*TLB*) are taken from *The Living Bible* © 1971. Used by permission of Tyndale House Publishers, Inc., Wheaton, IL 60189. All rights reserved.

Scripture taken from *THE MESSAGE: The Bible in Contemporary Language* © 2002 by Eugene H. Peterson. All rights reserved.

All rights reserved, including the right to reproduce this book, or any portions thereof, in any form. No part of this book may be reproduced or transmitted in any form or by any means, electronic or mechanical, magnetic, chemical, optical, manual, or otherwise, including photocopying, recording, or by any information storage or retrieval system without written permission from Richard A. Brott. All rights for publishing this book or portions thereof in other languages are contracted by the author.

This publication is designed to provide interesting reading material and general information with regard to the subject matter covered. It is printed, distributed and sold with the understanding that neither the publisher nor the author is engaged in rendering religious, family, legal, accounting, business, investing, financial, credit, debt or other professional advice. If any such advice is required, the services of a competent professional person should be sought. In summary, the content contained herein is not given as advice, rather it is strictly for the purpose of your reading entertainment.

Every effort has been made to supply complete and accurate information. However, neither the publisher nor the author assumes any responsibility for its use, nor for any infringements of patents or other rights of third parties that would result.

**First Edition, January 1, 2008**
Richard A. Brott
All Rights Reserved

# About the Author

Rich Brott holds a Bachelor of Science degree in Business and Economics and a Master of Business Administration.

Rich has served in an executive position of some very successful businesses. He has functioned on the board of directors for churches, businesses, and charities and served on a college advisory board. Rich has traveled to more than 25 countries on teaching assignments and business concerns.

He has authored thirty-five books including:

- *5 Simple Keys to Financial Freedom*
- *10 Life-Changing Attitudes That Will Make You a Financial Success*
- *15 Biblical Responsibilities Leading to Financial Wisdom*
- *30 Biblical Principles for Managing Your Money*
- *35 Keys to Financial Independence*
- *A Biblical Perspective On Giving Generously*
- *A Biblical Perspective On Tithing Faithfully*
- *A Biblical Perspective On Tithing & Giving*
- *Achieving Financial Alignment*
- *Activating Your Personal Faith to Receive*
- *All the Financial Scriptures in the Bible*
- *Basic Principles for Business Success*
- *Basic Principles for Developing Personal and Business Vision*
- *Basic Principles for Managing a Successful Business*
- *Basic Principles for Maximizing Your Personal Cash Flow*
- *Basic Principles for Starting a Successful Business*
- *Basic Principles of Conservative Investing*

- *Biblical Principles for Achieving Personal Success*
- *Biblical Principles for Becoming Debt Free*
- *Biblical Principles for Building a Successful Business*
- *Biblical Principles for Financial Success - Student Workbook*
- *Biblical Principles for Financial Success - Teacher Workbook*
- *Biblical Principles for Personal Evangelism*
- *Biblical Principles for Releasing Financial Provision*
- *Biblical Principles for Staying Out of Debt*
- *Biblical Principles for Success in Personal Finance*
- *Biblical Principles That Create Success Through Productivity*
- *Business, Occupations, Professions & Vocations In the Bible*
- *Family Finance Handbook*
- *Family Finance Student Workbook*
- *Family Finance Teacher Workbook*
- *How To Receive Prosperity & Provision*
- *Prosperity Has a Purpose*
- *Public Relations for the Local Church*
- *Successful Time Management*

He and his wife Karen, have been married for 36 years. Rich Brott resides in Portland, Oregon, with his wife, three children, son-in-law and granddaughter.

# Dedication

To all whom God has smiled upon and poured out His blessings and provision. May you in turn, help others.

# Table of Contents

Dedication ........................................................................5

Introduction ....................................................................9

*Principle 1:* The Principle of Understanding the
Importance of Right Decisions ...............................11

*Principle 2:* The Principle of Understanding the
Purpose of Financial Blessing .............................19

*Principle 3:* The Principle of You Are Blessed to Become a Blessing ...........23

*Principle 4:* The Principle of You Are Blessed for a Purpose .....................25

*Principle 5:* The Principle of You Are Blessed to
Become Faithful in Small Things .............................27

*Principle 6:* The Principle of You Have Been Chosen
for a Purpose Chosen by God.............................31

*Principle 7:* The Principle of God's Plan with Your Name on It.................35

*Principle 8:* The Principle of Acknowledging God's Ownership ..............41

*Principle 9:* The Principle of Being a Blessing .........................49

*Principle 10:* The Principle of Caring for a Brother ..................51

*Principle 11:* The Principle of Feeding the Local Church .......................53

*Principle 12:* The Principle of Finding Your Treasure ......................55

*Principle 13:* The Principle of The First Fruits...........................57

*Principle 14:* The Principle of Unending Gratitude ......................59

*Principle 15:* The Principle of Honoring the Lord With Your Wealth .......61

*Principle 16:* The Principle of Hospitality and Kindness ......................67

*Principle 17:* The Principle of Knowing That God Controls It All............75

*Principle 18:* The Principle of Knowing the Origin .....................77

*Principle 19:* The Principle of Lacking Absolutely Nothing ..........79

*Principle 20:* The Principle of Laying Up Treasures....................81

*Principle 21:* The Principle of Learning Real Success ..................83

*Principle 22:* The Principle of Lending to the Lord ....................85

*Principle 23:* The Principle of Putting Your Needs Last...............87

*Principle 24:* The Principle of Plenty Left Over..........................89

*Principle 25:* The Principle of Refreshing Others
                and Being Refreshed.............................................91

*Principle 26:* The Principle of Sharing Your Blessing...................93

*Principle 27:* The Principle of The Ultimate Gift.......................95

Summary .......................................................................99

Scriptures on Wealth, Riches and Prosperity.....................101

Scriptures on God's Provision and Abundance ..................137

Scriptures on Financial Topics...........................................153

Source Material................................................................255

# Introduction

**Proverbs 11:24–28**

*One man gives freely, yet gains even more; another withholds unduly, but comes to poverty.*

We gain by giving. We lose by withholding! You may recall the story about the widow and her son who were about to eat their last meal, as noted in 1 Kings 17. After that, they assumed they would just starve to death because they had no more food available, and there was a famine in the land. In our culture today, this is very hard for many of us to comprehend.

Some people teach that we should give to get. Others teach that we should sacrifice and withhold from our family in order to give more. Neither extreme point of view is correct. We must provide for our family. We should not give to get. Our attitude should be one of obedience and liberality. The best way to give to the Lord is to understand all that He has given to us, and then freely give back to Him.

God withholds His blessings from those who refuse to give. He cannot bless an act of disobedience. Our money becomes a curse when we think more of it than we do of God. One of the greatest privileges God has allowed us is to participate in the blessing of regular tithing and the giving of offerings.

When we freely give to God, regardless of our own personal need, we allow God to be big in our lives. We allow Him to provide for us. This can only happen as we buy into the principle of freely giving. If we are stingy in our giving and withhold from the Lord, we miss the many blessings and provisions He wants to shower upon us.

# Principle 1

## The Principle of
## Understanding the
## Importance of Right Decisions

*I*n the Gospels we read about four different individuals who all faced provision issues that required decisions about money. Let's take a look at each person and the life-changing, eternity-affecting decisions they made.

## The Ruthless Rich Man

### Luke 16:19–31

*"There was a rich man who was dressed in purple and fine linen and lived in luxury every day. At his gate was laid a beggar named Lazarus, covered with sores and longing to eat what fell from the rich man's table. Even the dogs came and licked his sores. The time came when the beggar died and the angels carried him to Abraham's side. The rich man also died and was buried. In hell, where he was in torment, he looked up and saw Abraham far away, with Lazarus by his side. So he called to him, 'Father Abraham, have pity on me and send Lazarus to dip the tip of his finger in water and cool my tongue, because I am in agony in this fire.'*

*But Abraham replied, 'Son, remember that in your lifetime you received your good things, while Lazarus received bad things, but now he is comforted here and you are in agony. And besides all this, between us and you a great chasm has been fixed, so that those who want to go from here to you cannot, nor can anyone cross over from there to us.' He answered, 'Then I beg you, father, send Lazarus to my father's house, for I have five brothers. Let him warn them, so that they will not also come to this place of torment.' Abraham replied, 'They have Moses and the Prophets; let them listen to them.'*

*'No, father Abraham,' he said, 'but if someone from the dead goes to them, they will repent.' He said to him, 'If they do not listen to Moses and the Prophets, they will not be convinced even if someone rises from the dead.'"*

The poor beggar by the name of Lazarus was left to die at the gate of the rich man, without food to nourish him and keep him alive. All he wanted were the mere crumbs that fell from the rich man's table, yet the rich man who lived in luxury refused to come to his aid or meet his need for mere survival.

Our culture and society have sold us a bill of goods. They teach us that in order to be happy, we have to have certain things. But we must resist the world's view of wealth, happiness, and possessions. We don't have to have it all! We don't have to wear just the right clothes, drive that certain brand of car, have the latest model available, buy a bigger home, own six televisions, possess the latest digital camera, and carry a dozen credit cards in our wallet.

We must not allow our culture to dictate to us its worldview of what our lives should consist of. Our society should not be allowed to design our lifestyle, nor should it tell us what success is and what the picture of affluence should look like. Success is doing what God wants done.

Wealth is having only what you need to exist. A rich man or woman is one who has one penny more than he or she needs. But wealth is more than money. It is having a local church that inspires you to draw close to God. It is having a loving spouse and the blessing of children. Wealth is enjoying great health and great relationships. Wealth is having good friends. Wealth is receiving salvation and God's gift of eternal life with Him.

# The Foolish Rich Man

### Luke 12:16–21

*And he told them this parable: "The ground of a certain rich man produced a good crop. He thought to himself, 'What shall I do? I have no place to store my crops.' Then he said, 'This is what I'll do. I will tear down my barns and build bigger ones, and there I will store all my grain and my goods. And I'll say to myself, "You have plenty of good things laid up for many years. Take life easy; eat, drink and be merry."'*

*"But God said to him, 'You fool! This very night your life will be demanded from you. Then who will get what you have prepared for yourself?' This is how it will be with anyone who stores up things for himself but is not rich toward God."*

This man apparently thought he would live forever...or at least a very long time. After storing up wealth for a long time (hoarding), he was planning to take his ease. Luke 12:15 instructs us to be on guard against every form of greed. It says that even when we have abundance, our lives are not to be caught up in our possessions.

Much of Western culture is centered around things and possessions that money can buy. Christian culture in the West is not immune to its influence. It's not that we are necessarily in love with money, but certainly we could say that we are enticed, maybe entrapped, by what we know money can do for us. Of course, we do live in this society and in this world's system, and we should not be so unwise as to think that we are immune from it altogether.

The Bible has a lot to say about material goods and our desire for them. The apostle Paul suggests that contentment is a very powerful value for guide us. Then he reminds us that we came into this world with nothing and will depart in the same way. He suggests that we should be happy when we have food to eat and clothes to wear. He notes that people who desire to get rich quickly often fall into temptation, fulfilling harmful desires that lead to ruin and destruction.

# The Greedy Rich Young Ruler

### Matthew 19:16–24

*Now a man came up to Jesus and asked, "Teacher, what good thing must I do to get eternal life?"*

*"Why do you ask me about what is good?" Jesus replied. "There is only One who is good. If you want to enter life, obey the commandments." "Which ones?" the man inquired. Jesus replied, "Do not murder, do not commit adultery, do not steal, do not give false testimony, honor your father and mother,' and 'love your neighbor*

*as yourself.'" "All these I have kept," the young man said. "What do I still lack?"*

*Jesus answered, "If you want to be perfect, go, sell your possessions and give to the poor, and you will have treasure in heaven. Then come, follow me." When the young man heard this, he went away sad, because he had great wealth. Then Jesus said to his disciples, "I tell you the truth, it is hard for a rich man to enter the kingdom of heaven. Again I tell you, it is easier for a camel to go through the eye of a needle than for a rich man to enter the kingdom of God."*

So many people today are on a quest to accumulate possessions and wealth. It is hard for all of us to be content with what we have when the world's entire system is geared toward making us unhappy with everything we have and desirous of everything we don't have. From advertising to attitude, we face a discontented culture.

How much money do we want to be content? Usually *just a little bit more.* But money cannot buy contentment or happiness. It is very hard for us to be satisfied with what we have, but we need to strive for contentment and contend for happiness. There is certainly nothing wrong with making money, so long as making money does not violate the laws of our land and the principles of God's Word. The all-for-me and none-for-others way of thinking is immoral. The person of principle who subscribes to the values of the Bible will be a good steward who obeys the law of giving. This person will find happiness in exact proportion to the degree he gives. He will be content with his life and all that it affords.

The story in Matthew 19 is the history of one who was a great young man, a good man, and it seems a principled man. He belonged to the ruling class of his time in history. But even in his culture, he was apparently influenced by a society of peers involved in hoarding finances. Because his possessions and personal wealth were substantial, he made a choice to hang on to what he had. Instead of being the conduit God intended, the receiving vessel thought it all belonged to him. The love of money, representing personal greed, kept him from following Christ.

The lesson learned here can really be summed up with a few questions: Are you satisfied with temporary treasure on earth, or are you preparing for eternal treasures in the life hereafter? Do you hold money, wealth, and possessions for the purpose of blessing others, or do the money, wealth, and assets that God has trusted you with have a hold on you?

## The Compassionate Rich Man

### Luke 10:30–37

In reply Jesus said: "A man was going down from Jerusalem to Jericho, when he fell into the hands of robbers. They stripped him of his clothes, beat him and went away, leaving him half dead. A priest happened to be going down the same road, and when he saw the man, he passed by on the other side. So too, a Levite, when he came to the place and saw him, passed by on the other side. But a Samaritan, as he traveled, came where the man was; and when he saw him, he took pity on him. He went to him and bandaged his wounds, pouring on oil and wine. Then he put the man on his own donkey, took him to an inn and took care of him. The next day he took out two silver coins and gave them to the innkeeper. 'Look after him,' he said, 'and when I return, I will reimburse you for any extra expense you may have.'

"Which of these three do you think was a neighbor to the man who fell into the hands of robbers?" The expert in the law replied, "The one who had mercy on him." Jesus told him, "Go and do likewise."

Better known to us as the Good Samaritan, the person in this story used the resources entrusted to him by God to help someone in need. The story of the Good Samaritan is the story of the integrity of a steward. Stewardship means that God owns you and is counting on you to become an instrument through which He can love and save the world. It's as simple as that! If you cannot offer yourself as a channel of God's wealth, how can He bless your life? The bottom line in stewardship is not money or a block of time, but your entire life and how you respond to those in need whose paths you cross.

Here are three thought-provoking questions for your consideration:

1. *Where are you placing your treasures?*

2. *Do you identify with the ruthless, the foolish, the greedy, or the compassionate use of God's blessing?*

3. *Will you be a conduit or channel through which blessings surge or a dam that stops the flow of the blessing of God?*

These are very candid, tough questions—were you satisfied with your answers?

# Principle 2

## The Principle of
## Understanding the
## Purpose of Financial Blessing

**N**othing happens in the economy of God until you give something away. It is a universal law of God. Paul very appropriately reminds us: "Remember this: Whoever sows sparingly will also reap sparingly, and whoever sows generously will also reap generously" (2 Corinthians 9:6).

Giving is the trigger for God's financial miracles. When you give to the Kingdom of God, it will be given back to you. But where will it come from? Who will give to you? Will God cause money to float down from heaven so that your needs are met? No. The Bible says, "Shall men give into your…[life]" (Luke 6:38, kjv). This is how the cycle of blessing works. When you give to God, He in turn causes others to give to you. Perhaps it will be in the form of new customers to your business, new products to sell, and so on. When God owns your business, He will make sure it prospers.

Scripture illustrates that giving of one's own things is evidence of God's grace in a person's life (2 Corinthians 8:4–7). Because 100 percent of what is received comes from God, we are responsible to use it wisely and in accordance with God's will. Like every other area of stewardship, God is interested in the whole picture, not just a percentage. What a person does with all his treasure is important to God.

The Good Samaritan was a trustee of God's provision. The person who takes stewardship seriously will regard his or her life, talents, strength, and money as a trust from God. Trustees have specific re-sponsibilities. They are charged with "holding property in trust" for someone else. Scriptural principles give us clues as to how we can trust God with our money and our entire life.

### 1 Timothy 6:17–19

*Command those who are rich in this present world not to be arrogant nor to put their hope in wealth, which is so uncertain, but to put their hope in God, who richly provides us with everything for our enjoyment. Command them to do good, to be rich in good deeds, and to be generous and willing to share. In this way they will lay up treasure for themselves as a firm foundation for the coming age, so that they may take hold of the life that is truly life.*

### Matthew 6:19–21

*"Do not store up for yourselves treasures on earth, where moth and rust destroy, and where thieves break in and steal. But store up for yourselves treasures in heaven, where moth and rust do not destroy, and where thieves do not break in and steal. For where your treasure is, there your heart will be also."*

What we care about, we invest in. If we invest our provision in the things God is interested in, our attitude will be the same. We will be interested in the ministry advance of our local church and will pray for the expansion of His kingdom locally and globally. Note that Jesus is not saying to have nothing, or enjoy nothing. Nor does

He imply any kind of sin. Christ is telling us not to get too tied to these things.

Be a conduit, not a dam. It's not about what we have, but what has us. If we center our life around our things and base our living upon our possessions, we will surely be disappointed. Don't base your life, your future, your well-being, or your happiness on the things you have accumulated. Instead, be sure that you lay up for yourself the real treasures, the ones that will be of eternal value.

## Financial Blessing

In this manuscript, you will encounter the words *blessed, blessing,* and *provision.* What do these words mean? How should they be applied within the confines of the text? From the beginning, let me give to you some insight into their meaning as applied in this book.

Some definitions are as follows, taken from *Roget's New Millennium Thesaurus*, First Edition: The word *blessing* is both a noun and a verb with a total of twenty-seven entries/definitions. The word *blessed* had twenty-four entries: as a noun, a verb, and adjective.

To be blessed in the human sense is to be happy, blissful, contented, fortunate, joyful, redeemed, saved, welcome, commendable, to be privileged, to possess, to not be in lack, need, or want, and to be favored. In the context of this book, *blessed* will be used in this way: to not be in lack or want, to be favored.

To have *blessing* or to be a *blessing* in our world is to have grace, reason for thanksgiving, asset, benefit, bounty, endorsement, gifts, fortune, godsend, help, kindness, miracle, profit, windfall, convenience, expediency, gain, influence, preference, prestige, permission, protection, recognition, resources, return, support, to invoke divine favor upon, treasure, and value. Within the pages of this book, the word *blessing* is used in this way: to experience the grace of God's influence, protection, resources, and assistance.

*Provision* in the dictionary is the "act of providing or making previous preparation…a stock of necessary supplies." Using a thesaurus, the following descriptions apply: allotment, allowance, apportionment, appropriation, equipping, fitting out, foundation, furnishing, keep, livelihood, living, maintenance, prearrangement, preparation, procurement, providing, reserve, supplying, subsistence, sustenance, and upkeep. The word *provision* will be applied as meaning: the supernatural appropriation of God's divine supply.

# Principle 3

## The Principle of
## You Are Blessed to Become a Blessing

A s direct as possible, here's why God allows many to become prosperous: You are blessed or will be blessed so that you can be a blessing to others. God does not prosper you for the purpose of raising your standard of living; He prospers you so that you can raise your standard of giving.

**Genesis 12:2**

> *And I will make of you a great nation, and I will bless you, and make your name great, so that you will be a blessing. (rsv)*

The call of God upon Abraham can be the model for God's call to us. Just as God promised to bless Abraham, He also will bless us. Why does God desire to bless His people? So that we might become a blessing to others.

**2 Corinthians 9:8**

> *And God is able to provide you with every blessing in abundance, so that you may always have enough of*

*everything and may provide in abundance for every good work. (rsv)*

Biblical stewardship is not about giving a lot of money just so the church can function in its community role. Yes, the church does need financing for its operational needs and vision mandate. But your role in receiving the supernatural provision of God is about keeping only a needed portion of God's blessing and returning a great portion of the blessing so that others can be blessed as well. We become resourceful and efficient stewards of all the possessions God has sent our way.

When it comes to the nonmonetary resources we have, such as our personal time, biblical stewardship is not about twisting arms and attempting to persuade people to volunteer for needed services. Rather it is about helping people recognize their God-given talents and abilities and helping them move into the giftings they have been blessed with. Once talents have been discovered and giftings acknowledged, it becomes the job of the church to figure out how those personal gifts can be utilized. It's not about volunteerism, but it is about gift mobilization.

# Principle 4

## The Principle of
## You Are Blessed for a Purpose

## People Blessed for a Purpose

Men and women of biblical times, historical times, and living today have been and continue to be blessed by God for a particular purpose. God has a purpose for our life; He will bring it to pass. Joseph was a man of humility, God-given talent, and wisdom and a person of purpose. As he submitted his life to the authority of the Almighty, the blessing of God was disbursed through his life and his hands.

### Genesis 39:1–5

*Now Joseph had been taken down to Egypt. And Potiphar, an officer of Pharaoh, captain of the guard, an Egyptian, bought him from the Ishmaelites who had taken him down there. The Lord was with Joseph, and he was a successful man; and he was in the house of his master the Egyptian. And his master saw that the Lord was with him and that the Lord made all he did to prosper in his hand. So Joseph found favor in his sight, and served him. Then he made him overseer of his house, and all that he had he put under his authority.*

*So it was, from the time that he had made him overseer of his house and all that he had, that the Lord blessed the Egyptian's house for Joseph's sake; and the blessing of the Lord was on all that he had in the house and in the field. (nkjv)*

**Genesis 41:40–43**

*"You shall be over my house, and all my people shall be ruled according to your word; only in regard to the throne will I be greater than you." And Pharaoh said to Joseph, "See, I have set you over all the land of Egypt." Then Pharaoh took his signet ring off his hand and put it on Joseph's hand; and he clothed him in garments of fine linen and put a gold chain around his neck. And he had him ride in the second chariot which he had; and they cried out before him, "Bow the knee!" So he set him over all the land of Egypt. (nkjv)*

What would happen to the vision of the Church if all Christians yielded their lives as Joseph did and became instruments through which God's blessing flowed? I believe it is time once again for God's people to prosper in the land like Joseph of old.

# Principle 5

## The Principle of
## You Are Blessed to
## Become Faithful in Small Things

**W**hat is the level of your faithfulness? Are you asking God for great provision while being unfaithful in the smaller blessings He has allowed to come your way? Joseph, after being sold by his brothers into slavery, suffered a great injustice and could have easily turned his back on God and become a very bitter person. But Joseph provides us with a good example. In spite of all the bad things wished upon him by his half-brothers, he still remained strong because he believed in God.

The special talents and gifts possessed by Joseph were not only intellectual, but also moral. He had been faithful in that which was little and therefore was qualified to be faithful in much. It didn't matter whether it was his brothers, Potiphar (his new master), the jailer, the other prisoners, or Pharaoh, Joseph was determined to serve others well. He believed and did not doubt that everything that had happened to him was in the divine plan of God. He believed that God had a definite plan and purpose for his life.

In Egypt, Joseph threw himself with goodwill into his duties as a slave. Though he had wept and pleaded with his brothers when they sold him, once he was taken away, he showed no sign of murmuring or complaint. When we find ourselves cut off from our hopes and dreams, as Joseph was, we can still look ahead and believe that God is on the throne and that His promises will not fail.

God honored Joseph for his faithfulness and helped him to be successful in everything he was assigned to do. God's blessing upon Joseph was not only noticed, but also impressed his master. After a time, Potiphar (an Egyptian officer, captain of the guard for Pharaoh) made him the overseer and manager of his household and all his possessions.

When God began to deal with Joseph, we see not just one test, but test after test. Because of his walk with the Lord, the severity of Joseph's trials, instead of discouraging him, strengthened and purified him. Potiphar's wife, angered by Joseph's purity, accused him falsely. Soon Joseph was in prison with no hope of release. Slaves had no rights. Joseph accepted this in silence, not once accusing his master's wife or attempting to justify or defend himself in any way.

Through all of this trouble, Joseph continued to honor and trust God. At the same time, he gave himself freely to do whatever he was asked to do. Even the prison keeper could not help but recognize that Joseph was different and deserved his confidence. Joseph did not choose to be cast into prison, but when he found himself there, he used every bit of energy and ability he had to do the best work he could. He never shrank from responsibility even under the most adverse conditions and circumstances.

He could have taken the attitude, "I'm in prison and what can a man do for God in prison? How can I possibly be blessed, let alone bless others? I'll just wait until God gets me out."

If we wait for perfect conditions, we will never do the work God wants us to do.

Ecclesiastes 9:10 says, "Whatsoever thy hand findeth to do, do it with thy might" (kjv). God has a way of accomplishing His will, and every time His will is fulfilled, He receives the glory!

Because of Joseph's faithfulness in carrying out his duties, Pharaoh eventually noticed him and gave him great power. Genesis 41:41 states, "So Pharaoh said to Joseph, 'I hereby put you in charge of the whole land of Egypt.'" After a series of events, Joseph had the opportunity to forgive his brothers and provide financial aid and blessing to his entire family. God fully vindicated Joseph's faith. After all the years of adversity, God's purpose was accomplished.

Genesis 50:20 sums up Joseph's attitude: "You intended to harm me, but God intended it for good to accomplish what is now being done, the saving of many lives."

# Principle 6

## The Principle of
## You Have Been Chosen for a Purpose

## Chosen by God

**Ephesians 1:4–5**

> *For he chose us in him before the creation of the world to be holy and blameless in his sight. In love he predestined us to be adopted as his sons through Jesus Christ, in accordance with his pleasure and will.*

Notice how we are viewed by the Almighty. This Scripture says that we were *chosen*. God has chosen us! In His great mercy and love, God reached down and offered us a better way of living. God, who created the universe; God, who flung the stars into space; God, who placed the sun and the moon into position... Think about it—just as God chose Joseph of old, the God of the heavenlies chose us!

Hundreds of years ago, our forefathers needed a national point of reference for the country. They knew the new country needed to be surveyed. In America, the first iron stake was driven in the northeastern seaboard. So it was with God. He established for us a point of reference. He has given to us a sense of destiny.

According to Romans 8:29, "For whom He did foreknow, he also did *predestinate*" (kjv). Predestinate means to design, to purpose, to contemplate, to expect, and to anticipate. Since God knew that one day you would be tender toward the Lord, He just went ahead and included you in His divine blueprint and planned some things for you to do in the great design of His eternal will.

God did not force His will upon you. You were free to make your own decisions. But He did know what your response to the gospel would be, so He designed some of His blueprint with each of you in mind. He has included you and has marked out a place for you on the drawing boards of eternity. You see, before God even created the world, He designed His kingdom with each of you in mind.

## Chosen for a Specific Purpose

**Ephesians 1:11**

> *In whom also we have obtained an inheritance, being predestinated according to the purpose of him who worketh all things after the counsel of his own will. (kjv)*

Purpose is the key to all of God's will. Purpose determines the rightness and wrongness of any action. Purpose determines the usefulness of any object or person. The greatest gift Christ gave His disciples was a sense of purpose: a knowledge that they had a responsibility to fulfill and a role to play in the kingdom of God.

It caused them to lay everything aside and to dedicate themselves to doing the divine will of God. The disciples worked in many different occupations of life. They seemed to be lost in their world, some wandering and all living in a vacuum. But when Jesus Christ stepped into their lives, He gave them a sense of worth and direction.

He said to His disciples, "You didn't choose me, but I chose you. I picked you out and brought you into My kingdom." He said to Peter, "I'm going to make you a fisher of men." He said to Matthew, "Do you remember where I found you...sitting at the feet of custom? You were glaring back at people just as hatefully as they were glaring at you. You told them to put their money on the table or you would call the soldiers to take them away. Matthew, there was hatred all around you and that's the kind of atmosphere I took you out of."

Some of you reading this book lived in a world of hate until Jesus found you. Some of you never knew real love until you met Jesus. If I could pull up a chair next to you and ask you where God found you, you would tell me about various backgrounds and stories of life. You might tell me of the dark pit of debt and poverty you once found yourself in. Then perhaps you would tell me about how God began to bless your life, your family, your business, and your financial world. Have you ever stopped to think about why His supernatural provision is upon you or why you think it should be upon you?

The Lord is saying to you this day as you are reading this page that He picked you out of the terrible world that you lived in and loved you just as you were and where you were and said, "I choose you!" He is saying to you, "I'll do things for you...I'll build you into a better person than what you are. I am going to give to you a sense of purpose and a future, and I will bring that future into your life." Purpose was given to the disciples of Christ and purpose has been given to you!

You have been chosen to work out something in God's divine will.

# Principle 7

## The Principle of
## God's Plan with Your Name on It

## God Has a Plan Designed with Your Name on It

**Jeremiah 29:11**

> *"For I know the plans I have for you...plans to prosper you and not to harm you, plans to give you hope and a future"*

Christ has chosen you! He has given you a sense of your ultimate destiny. Back in the recesses of time, long before your encounter with God, He had you in mind. God knew that someday you would be exposed to the gospel. He also knew just how you would respond to the spoken and written Word of God.

Since God knew this, He included you in His plan and fixed something for you to do in the great design of His eternal will. Since your Creator knew that your personal reaction to the gospel would be favorable, He designed His great plan with you in mind. He made room for one more new Christian and continued to prepare a place for you on the drawing board of eternity.

Because one day we took a step toward Christ, we were given a new perspective on life. Before there ever was a star in the sky, He planned out and fixed a niche for you to fit and work within. He willed that you, as a Christian filled with the Holy Spirit, be involved in and do some of His divine work. He has a purpose and place for you in His kingdom!

## Abraham's Blessing

**Genesis 12:1–4**

> *Now [in Haran] the Lord said to Abram, Go for yourself [for your own advantage] away from your country, from your relatives and your father's house, to the land that I will show you. And I will make of you a great nation, and I will bless you [with abundant increase of favors] and make your name famous and distinguished, and you will be a blessing [dispensing good to others]. And I will bless those who bless you [who confer prosperity or happiness upon you] and curse him who curses or uses insolent language toward you; in you will all the families and kindred of the earth be blessed [and by you they will bless themselves]. So Abram departed, as the Lord had directed him; and Lot [his nephew] went with him. Abram was seventy-five years old when he left Haran. (amp)*

The father of many nations, at the ripe old age of seventy-five, listened to the call and voice of God. In exchange for his obedience, he was promised the "blessed" life. His life stands as a model for each of us today.

### Show You

The Lord tells Abraham that He will "show" him the land of blessing, prosperity, and provision. What is God showing you? What dreams, ideas, and visions have you had?

### Make You

The Lord told Abraham that He will "make" something out of his obedience. What is God desiring to make out of your life of obedience?

### Bless You

The Lord told Abraham that He would "bless" him. The Amplified Bible explains this to be an "abundant increase of favors." Abraham's greatness was to be because of God. The greatness you seek should not be sought outside of the presence and power of God. It is achieved not because of you but because of God in you. The blessings and supernatural provision come in all forms. What do yours look like? Are you grateful for and do you recognize all the blessings God has given you?

### Bless Those

Finally, the Lord God told Abraham that He would "bless those who bless you." Those he would encounter, who would confer prosperity and happiness upon him, would see the same blessing come upon their own life. God desires to bless all who are obedient to His Word.

## Abram (Abraham) Departed

In obedience to God, Abram packed up his belongings and headed on down the road. Was Abram chosen because of his good works? Did he have a good heart? Was it just because he was a special person? No! God wants to bless all of His children! Abraham's life is highlighted in Scripture because of his faith in the ultimate provision of God. Numbers 6:24–26 makes it clear that the blessing of God is for all. "The Lord bless you and keep you; the Lord make his face shine upon you and be gracious to you; the Lord turn his face toward you and give you peace."

Why does God want to bless you? His purpose in blessing you is so you can turn around and bless others! Who are we to bless? Our family and friends and those who can repay us? The children? The sick and the needy? The poor and down-and-out? Yes, it is easy to bless all of the above. Jesus said this in Matthew 25:34–40:

> *"Then the King will say to those on his right, 'Come, you who are blessed by my Father; take your inheritance, the kingdom prepared for you since the creation of the world. For I was hungry and you gave me something to eat, I was thirsty and you gave me something to drink, I was a stranger and you invited me in, I needed clothes and you clothed me, I was sick and you looked after me, I was in prison and you came to visit me.' Then the righteous will answer him, 'Lord, when did we see you hungry and feed you, or thirsty and give you something to drink? When did we see you a stranger and invite you in, or needing clothes and clothe you? When did we see you sick or in prison and go to visit you?' The King will reply, 'I tell you the truth, whatever you did for one of the least of these brothers of mine, you did for me.'"*

But Jesus also said for us to bless those who curse us, mistreat us, and are against us. This is much harder for us to do, yet Jesus commanded us to do so.

**Luke 6:27–37**

*"But I tell you who hear me: Love your enemies, do good to those who hate you, bless those who curse you, pray for those who mistreat you. If someone strikes you on one cheek, turn to him the other also. If someone takes your cloak, do not stop him from taking your tunic. Give to everyone who asks you, and if anyone takes what belongs to you, do not demand it back. Do to others as you would have them do to you. If you love those who love you, what credit is that to you? Even 'sinners' love those who love them. And if you do good to those who are good to you, what credit is that to you? Even 'sinners' do that. And if you lend to those from whom you expect repayment, what credit is that to you? Even 'sinners' lend to 'sinners,' expecting to be repaid in full. But love your enemies, do good to them, and lend to them without expecting to get anything back. Then your reward will be great, and you will be sons of the Most High, because he is kind to the ungrateful and wicked. Be merciful, just as your Father is merciful."*

## Blessed for a Purpose

For every person, He has a purpose. And that purpose is ultimately that you might become a blessing to others. That as God supernaturally provides for you, you in turn will not be one who dams up the river of blessing, but one who becomes a conduit so the blessings flow to others. Are you living in the purpose of God? Are you operating in the plan He designed for your life? Are you giving to others as you are blessed yourself? Wherever you go, be a blessing! With whomever you meet, become a blessing! Whatever you put your hand to, be a blessing! You have been blessed for a purpose!

# Principle 8

## The Principle of
## Acknowledging God's Ownership

**A**re we the owners of our money and possessions, or is God? The correct answer is that *God owns it all*. As Creator of the world and owner of all it possesses, He is in complete control of everything. God owns the world. God owns me. God owns my money. God owns my possessions. He owns me because He created me. He owns me because He bought me again when He purchased me with His life. I need to acknowledge His ownership!

It is also true that if God owns it all, He has the right to control it all. If He has the right to control all, does He not also have the right to delegate some responsibility to us? The Bible calls us stewards. Our role today is that of managers. A steward or manager is someone who has been put in charge of possessions that he or she does not own.

If everything truly comes from God (and it does), then He owns it all. If He owns it all, then we have been placed in charge of possessions that belong to someone else. We, as stewards or managers, are accountable to the owner, God, for the quality of managing. What kind of results are we producing? How good of a money/possessions manager are you? Is there room for improvement?

# God Owns It All

What then belongs to God? Of course, the real personal struggle usually accompanies the money He allows to flow through our hands and the material possessions we often try to accumulate. It all comes from God.

# The Earth

### 1 Chronicles 29:13–14

*Our God, we thank thee.... For all things come of thee, and of thine own have we given thee. (kjv)*

### Exodus 9:29

*The earth is the Lord's.*

### Isaiah 66:1–2

*Thus saith the Lord, "The heaven is my throne, and the earth is my footstool: For all those things hath mine hand made." (kjv)*

### Acts 7:49–50

*Heaven is my throne, and earth is my footstool: Hath not my hand made all these things? (kjv)*

**2 Kings 19:15**

*Thou art the God...thou hast made heaven and earth.
(kjv)*

**Nehemiah 9:6**

*Thou, even thou, art Lord alone; thou hast made
heaven, the heaven of heavens, with all their host, the
earth, and all things that are therein, the seas, and all
that is therein, and thou preservest them all. (kjv)*

**Jeremiah 27:5**

*I have made the earth, the man and the beast that
are upon the ground, by my great power and by my
out-stretched arm, and have given it unto whom it
seemed meet unto me. (kjv)*

**Hebrews 1:10**

*And, thou, Lord, in the beginning hast laid the founda-
tion of the earth; and the heavens are the works of thine
hands. (kjv)*

**Acts 17:24**

*God that made the world and all things therein, seeing
that he is Lord of heaven and earth, dwelleth not in
temples made with hands. (kjv)*

## Job 12:9–10

*Who knoweth not in all these that the hand of the Lord hath wrought this? In whose hand is the soul [life] of every living thing, and the breath of all mankind. (kjv)*

## Psalm 89:11

*The heavens are thine, the earth also is thine: as for the world and the fullness thereof, thou hast founded them. (kjv)*

## Psalm 95:3, 5

*For the Lord is a great God.... The sea is his, for he made it, and his hands formed the dry land.*

## Daniel 4:17

*The most High ruleth in the kingdom of men, and giveth it to whomsoever he wills, and setteth up over it the basest of men. (kjv)*

## John 19:11

*Jesus answered, "Thou couldest have no power at all against me, except it were given thee from above." (kjv)*

**Revelation 4:11**

*Thou art worthy, O Lord, to receive glory and honour and power: for thou hast created all things, and for thy pleasure they are and were created. (kjv)*

# Our Possessions (Material and Money)

**1 Timothy 6:17–19**

*Command those who are rich in this present world not to be arrogant nor to put their hope in wealth, which is so uncertain, but to put their hope in God, who richly provides us with everything for our enjoyment. Command them to do good, to be rich in good deeds, and to be generous and willing to share. In this way they will lay up treasure for themselves as a firm foundation for the coming age, so that they may take hold of the life that is truly life.*

Note here that God "richly provides" us with everything for our enjoyment, but it does come with some conditions: to do good, be rich in good deeds, be generous, and be willing to share.

# Our Abilities

God gives us talents and abilities so that we can use them for His kingdom. We are accountable for His giftings.

**Romans 12:6–8**

*We have different gifts, according to the grace given us. If a man's gift is pro-phesying, let him use it in proportion to his faith. If it is serving, let him serve; if it is teaching, let him teach; if it is encouraging, let him encourage; if it is contributing to the needs of others, let him give generously; if it is leadership, let him govern diligently; if it is showing mercy, let him do it cheerfully.*

## Our Time

**Ephesians 5:15–16**

*Be very careful, then, how you live—not as unwise but as wise, making the most of every opportunity, because the days are evil.*

## Our Bodies

**1 Corinthians 6:19–20**

*Do you not know that your body is a temple of the Holy Spirit, who is in you, whom you have received from God? You are not your own; you were bought at a price. Therefore honor God with your body.*

### Romans 12:1–2

*Therefore, I urge you, brothers, in view of God's mercy, to offer your bodies as living sacrifices, holy and pleasing to God—this is your spiritual act of worship. Do not conform any longer to the pattern of this world, but be transformed by the renewing of your mind. Then you will be able to test and approve what God's will is—his good, pleasing and perfect will.*

Having the knowledge that God owns it all is the first step to becoming an honorable steward. It is crucial that you take a moment to reflect and confess to yourself and to God that He is in control and that you want to be a reputable steward of His possessions.

Although head knowledge and confession are good, it is more important that you live a lifestyle fulfilling this principle. These words should be embedded in your heart and its fruit exemplified in your daily decisions: what I do with my possessions reveals what is truly in my heart.

# Principle 9

## The Principle of
## Being a Blessing

**Genesis 12:2–3**

*I will make your name great, and you will be a bless-ing. I will bless those who bless you, and whoever curses you I will curse; and all peoples on earth will be blessed through you.*

Blessing others! Here is a great story about being a blessing to others. R. Braxton Hagele writes in the August 19, 1998 edition of Wit and Wisdom the following account:

One stormy night many years ago, an elderly man and his wife entered the lobby of a small hotel in Philadelphia. Trying to get out of the rain, the couple approached the front desk hoping to get some shelter for the night. "Could you possibly give us a room here?" the husband asked. The clerk, a friendly man with a winning smile, looked at the couple and explained that there were three conventions in town.

"All of our rooms are taken," the clerk said. "But I can't send a nice couple like you out into the rain at one o'clock in the morning. Would you perhaps be willing to sleep in my room? It's not exactly a suite, but it will be good enough to make you folks comfortable for the night." When the couple declined, the young man pressed on. "Don't worry about me; I'll make out just fine," the clerk told them. So the couple agreed. As he paid his bill the next morning, the elderly man said to the clerk, "You are the kind of manager who should be the boss of the best hotel in the United States. Maybe someday I'll build one for you."

The clerk looked at them and smiled. The three of them had a good laugh. As they drove away, the elderly couple agreed that the helpful clerk was indeed exceptional, as finding people who are both friendly and helpful isn't easy.

Two years passed. The clerk had almost forgotten the incident when he received a letter from the old man. It recalled that stormy night and enclosed a round-trip ticket to New York, asking the young man to pay them a visit.

The old man met him in New York, and led him to the corner of Fifth Avenue and 34th Street. He then pointed to a great new building, a palace of reddish stone, with turrets and watchtowers thrusting up to the sky. "That," said the older man, "is the hotel I have just built for you to manage."

"You must be joking," the young man said.

"I can assure you I am not," said the older man, a sly smile playing around his mouth.

The older man's name was William Waldorf Astor, and the magnificent structure was the original Waldorf-Astoria Hotel. The young clerk who became its first manager was George C. Boldt.

This young clerk never foresaw the turn of events that would lead him to become the manager of one of the world's most glamorous hotels. The Bible says that we are not to turn our backs on those who are in need, for we might be entertaining angels.

# Principle 10

## The Principle of
## Caring for a Brother

**1 John 3:17**

*But whoso hath this world's good, and seeth his brother have need, and shutteth up his bowels of compassion from him, how dwelleth the love of God in him? (kjv)*

A nineteenth-century folktale is set in a small town in Russia, where a terrible cold wave was causing extreme suffering to the poor. On one bitingly cold day, the rabbi went to solicit the only wealthy man in town, a man known to be a miser.

The rabbi knocked, and the man opened the door. "Come in, Rabbi," the rich man said. Unlike everyone else in town, he was only in shirtsleeves; after all, his house was well heated. "No," the rabbi said. "No need for me to come in. I'll just be a minute." The rabbi then proceeded to engage the rich man in a lengthy conversation, asking him detailed questions concerning each member of his family. The man was shivering, yet every time he asked the rabbi to come inside, the rabbi refused.

"And your wife's cousin, the lumber merchant, how is he?" the rabbi asked.

The rich man's cheeks were fiery red. "What did you come here for, Rabbi?"

"Oh, that," the rabbi said. "I need money from you to buy coal for the poor people in town."

"So why don't you come in and we'll talk about it?"

"Because if I come in, we will sit down by your fireplace. You will be very warm and comfortable, and when I tell you how the poor are suffering from the cold, you really won't understand. You'll give me five rubles, maybe ten, and send me away. But now, out here," the rabbi went on, indicating the frozen moisture on the man's cheeks, "when I tell you how the poor are suffering from the cold, I think you'll understand better. Right?"

The man was happy to give the rabbi one hundred rubles just so he could shut the door and return to his fireplace.1

# Principle 11

## The Principle of
## Feeding the Local Church

**Malachi 3:10**

*Bring the whole tithe into the storehouse, that there may be food in my house.*

I have met a number of people who adamantly propose that their tithe belongs to whomever they decide to give it. One longtime Christian who faithfully defends the cause believes that she is tithing when she gives money to her married children. Of course, there are many people with many needs. Then you have those who somehow drop into your life whether in person or via the media who have their hands out.

Help whomever you wish, but don't confuse the tithe with your other charitable giving. The tithe belongs to your local church. This is where you are fed, sustained, and have relationships. Only they will help you should you one day find yourself in need. Only your local church will see to it that you are visited in the hospital or fed when you are without. God's funding plan for the operation of the local church is His tithe, which comes from your increase.

# Principle 12

## The Principle of
## Finding Your Treasure

**Matthew 6:21**

*For where your treasure is, there your heart will be also.*
*(nkjv)*

God is not in the business of bringing supernatural provision to our lives so that we can heap luxury and desires upon ourselves for personal gratification.

The Scriptures are full of instructions about sacrificing, bringing offerings, and giving to the Lord. Jesus was not a fund-raiser, but He talked about stewardship a great deal. Jesus dealt with money matters, because money matters! Both God and Satan know that "where your treasure is, there your heart will be also." That's why both are very interested in what we do with our money. Our attitude toward money is a spiritual matter! If our attitude is right, we will give as needed, and by doing so an unending supply of provision will come our way.

What kind of a heart for giving do you have? Who does giving help, you or God? Does God need your money? Of course not! Do you need God's blessing? Certainly! Your giving is not an act of charity on your part, but rather an act of worship and obedience to God. It is a very real, very tangible acknowledgment that you are placing

God first in your life, that He is foremost in your thoughts, that He is whom you treasure in your heart.

When you treasure Him more than earthly treasures, here is the result: "And God is able to make all grace abound to you, so that in all things at all times, having all that you need, you will abound in every good work" (2 Corinthians 9:8–9). Observe the multiple use of the word all. It certainly does away with any limitations of God's favor upon your life.

# Principle 13

## The Principle of
## The First Fruits

**Proverbs 3:9–10**

*Honor the Lord with your possessions, and with the firstfruits of all your increase; So your barns will be filled with plenty, and your vats will overflow with new wine. (nkjv)*

**Exodus 13:1–2**

*The Lord said to Moses, "Consecrate to me every first-born male. The first offspring of every womb among the Israelites belongs to me, whether man or animal."*

What do you do with God's provision upon your life? Are you one that honors God with your money? Or are you a person who does not honor God but are generally good with handling your money? Perhaps, if neither of those descriptions fit you, maybe you just look like you are good with handling money, but are really on the brink of financial collapse and don't even know it. Or a different scenario might be that you are in a financial crisis and you know it.

These Scriptures show us how not to get into financial trouble. We stay out of trouble by first honoring the Lord with our possessions and by consecrating or giving from the firstfruits of our increase.

# Principle 14

## The Principle of
## Unending Gratitude

### Luke 17:11–18

> *As they continued onward toward Jerusalem, they
> reached the border between Galilee and Samaria, and
> as they entered a village there, ten lepers stood at a dis-
> tance, crying out, "Jesus, sir, have mercy on us!" He
> looked at them and said, "Go to the Jewish priest and
> show him that you are healed!" And as they were going,
> their leprosy disappeared. One of them came back to
> Jesus, shouting, "Glory to God, I'm healed!" He fell flat
> on the ground in front of Jesus, face downward in the
> dust, thanking him for what he had done. This man
> was a despised Samaritan. Jesus asked, "Didn't I heal
> ten men? Where are the nine?" (rsv)*

A very sad occasion in the life of Jesus occurred during His last
pilgrimage to Jerusalem. About to be totally rejected by the very
people He came to save, He now would minister to one more group
of ungrateful people.

This is the story of ten individuals, each carrying the dreadful
disease of leprosy. This was the planet's most terrible disease of that
time, characterized by paralyzed and deformed bodies.

In order for the healing process to be complete, Jesus gave them some personal instructions to carry out. They were to go present themselves to their priest. As they journeyed, something miraculous happened inside them. New life shot through their withered, corrupted frames. Their slow, halting steps became strong and firm. Solid, healthy flesh replaced the decay that had hung on their bones. All had been healed, all ten—no exceptions!

But sadly, only one of them had the decency to return to Jesus and express thankfulness. This humble one approached Jesus and slipped to his knees, crying, "Jesus, I am healed. I am grateful. I am thankful!"

The other nine never returned. God expects believers to be grateful people. The Word expresses this clearly: "Giving thanks always for all things" (Ephesians 5:20); "Abounding therein with thanksgiving" (Colossians 2:7); "Be ye thankful" (Colossians 3:15).

Gratitude is a Christian attitude. It is not the mark of a discontented person, rather one who has learned to be content with the blessings of God. Gratitude puts a cork in the bottle of covetousness. The envious person is a gloomy person, always envisioning those things that could be; whereas the grateful one savors those things that already exist.

The nine ungrateful lepers walked away with healthy bodies but with deformed souls. The thankful leper was not only cleansed of his physical illness, but he heard the Lord say that his faith had made him completely whole, mind, soul, and spirit!

# Principle 15

## The Principle of
## Honoring the Lord With Your Wealth

**Proverbs 3:9**

*Honor the Lord with your wealth.*

Many readers of this book would not think their lifestyle is one of wealth and excess. To you the words extravagant and excessive would not seem descriptive of your standard of living. But the reality is that most of us really do live a life of abundance. We travel where we wish, we buy what we desire, and there are very few constraints in our lifetime of opportunities.

Dr. Neil Chadwick explains how wealthy some of us really are in the country of my origin (USA) in this excerpt from one of his messages.

Recently it has come to my attention just how imbalanced a world we live in. The fact of the matter is, if you have food in the refrigerator, clothes on your back, a roof overhead and a place to sleep, you are richer than 75 percent of this world. If you have money in the bank, in your wallet, and spare change in a dish someplace—you are among the top 8 percent of the world's wealthy. If we could shrink the earth's population to a village of precisely 100 people, with all the existing human ratios remaining the same, 6 people would possess 59 percent of the entire world's wealth and all

6 would be from the United States; 80 would live in substandard housing; 70 would be unable to read; 50 would suffer from malnutrition; and only 1 would have a college education.

So what do you think about this verse in Proverbs 3:9: "Honor the Lord with your wealth"? Do you think it applies to someone else? Were you tempted to skip this principle, thinking it wasn't applicable to you? While the next few stories speak of individuals with great wealth, don't be so sure that when you compare your circumstances with historical data and the rest of the world today, you shouldn't take notice. Regardless of whether or not you have great wealth, by the standards of most of the world's citizens, you are a wealthy person.

## Paul White

BTD Manufacturing, Inc., a metal stamping and fabrication business, was established by Paul White and Earl Rasmussen. Their goal was to have a company that would always honor its greatest assets—its people. Along with that was a commitment to charitable giving. So the BTD Manufacturing Foundation was begun in the year 1988. The company's goal is to share the profits with people in need. A few years ago, Paul White also established his own donor-advised family fund named the White Family Foundation. The family's charitable interests are driven in large part by a belief that people of wealth are merely stewards of those dollars on behalf of God. He says, "God gave each of us specific gifts and talents. If we use these talents in earning dollars, then we need to share those dollars with others."

## Sir John Marks Templeton

Sir John Marks Templeton is a Rhodes scholar and a Yale graduate. Early in the forties, he began to try his hand in the art of investment. He established his first mutual fund in 1954. Using this fund, he purchased international equities long before other American investors did so. This first fund of his proved to be very successful. A typical investment of $10,000 in the year 1954 without additional contributions would have grown to a whopping $3 million by the year 1992. It was in 1992 that he sold his company for more than $400 million.

Mr. Templeton today remains a faith-filled, religious, values-oriented Christian philanthropist. He has been known to pay professors if they would promote conservative values. He gives to universities to build character in the lives of young persons. He funds researchers who will connect faith and science.

He launched the Templeton Prize for Progress in Religion in 1972. The first award went to Mother Teresa, some six years before she won the Nobel Peace Prize. Other winners include famous names as Billy Graham and Chuck Colson. In 2003, Mr. Templeton began the Templeton Honor Roll, which distinguished 126 universities, departments, professors, and textbooks that uphold conservative and traditional educational values.

## Andrew Carnegie

Andrew Carnegie was one of the leading industrialist of America's nineteenth century. Building America's steel industry made him one of the greatest and riches entrepreneurs in history. But it was not always that way. He was born in Scotland, to the son of a weaver in 1835, in a city that was the center of the linen industry. After the industrial revolution took place, the steam-powered looms put thousands of craftsman out of work. This caused his entire family to go to work selling groceries and mending shoes. Fearing future economic survival, the family borrowed enough money to travel by ship to North America. They took up residence in Pittsburgh, the iron-manufacturing center of the country.

Andrew's father found work in a cotton factory, and Andrew became a bobbin boy at a pay rate of $1.20 per week. From that job he went on to become a messenger boy in the local telegraph office. Later he began working at the Pennsylvania Railroad as a private secretary and personal telegrapher for a salary of around $35 per month. He once said, "I couldn't imagine what I could ever do with so much money." Excelling in his responsibilities, he soon became the superintendent of the Pittsburgh Division. During the Civil War he helped to supervise military transportation for the North. After the war he worked for the Keystone Bridge Company replacing wooden bridges with bridges built of iron. He began earning an annual income of $50,000.

Over the ensuing years he worked to convert iron to steel, using his own personal money and borrowing additional funds to build a new steel plant near Pittsburgh. His motto was "Watch costs and the profits take care of themselves." By 1900, his plant produced more steel than all plants in Great Britain. Financier J. P. Morgan sought to take over the Carnegie Steel Company and did so at a cost of $480 million, making Andrew Carnegie the richest man in the world.

In his book, *The Gospel of Wealth*, Andrew Carnegie talks about how change has come to this nation. He states:

> The poor enjoy what the rich could not before afford. What were the luxuries have become the necessaries of life. The laborer has now more comforts than the farmer had a few generations ago. The farmer has more luxuries than the landlord had, and is more richly clad and better housed. The landlord has books and pictures rarer and appointments more artistic than the king could then obtain.

He wrote this in the year 1889. I wonder what he would write today.

After spending a lifetime accumulating wealth and fortune, his later years were spent in giving it away to institutions of science, education, charitable foundations, libraries, churches, and culture. By the time of his death, he had donated approximately $350 million to various worthy causes. He often said, "The man who dies rich, dies disgraced." He used his money to help others help themselves.

## Myrna Rose Strand

Myrna Strand is a retired school teacher from Minneapolis who decided to give her estate to charitable causes. She says, "My estate will never be large enough to be able to build libraries, but it may be large enough to buy some books for a library." As a young girl, she was taught and willingly placed coins in the Sunday school offering envelope each week. Throughout her life she has been generous with her money and her time, volunteering thousands of hours to church and other charities. She continues, "I have always wanted the balance of my estate to go to charities. I believe in the idea that when you come into the world you come in with nothing, and you have an obligation to give back. You can't take it with you. I believe I should carefully manage the resources God has entrusted to me, to care for His world, His people, His creation, and myself."

God has blessed so many with great wealth, assets, and riches compared to just a generation or two ago. What are you doing with your blessing? Are you honoring God or yourself?

# Principle 16

## The Principle of
# Hospitality and Kindness

**Romans 12:13**

*Distributing to the necessity of saints; given to hospital-
ity. (kjv)*

Gander is a small town with a population of 10,500 people
that lies in the northeastern tip of North America. It is located in
the Atlantic province of Newfoundland, Canada. It is the location
of the largest international airport in that region. When refueling is
needed during transatlantic flights, Gander is the place to stop. On
that terrible day of September 11, 2001, when American airspace
was completely closed due to the terrorist attacks, Gander served
39 of the 120 U.S. bound transatlantic flights that were diverted to
Canada. These flights carried over 6,500 passengers.

If you wondered about all those flights that were in the middle
of the great blue Atlantic Ocean on the morning of September 11,
here is an up-close-and-personal story written by a Delta Airlines
flight attendant en route from Frankfurt to Atlanta.

On September 11, a Delta aircraft was loaded with passengers
and in-flight during the terrorist attack on the United States. With
all aircraft ordered to land immediately, the nearest possible landing
site was in Gander, Newfoundland, Canada.

Even though the residents of the town of Gander experienced a disruption of their own personal schedules, they went out of their way to house, feed, entertain, and serve the passengers of Delta Flight 15. Not only did they show great hospitality and kindness to this particular flight, many other airlines were also grounded and experienced the very same kindness from this town.

This is a true story which is told about the hospitality and kindness shown by the residents of the town of Gander in Newfoundland. It is said to have been written by a member of the crew by the name of Nazim-Amin, although research was unable to verify the writer unconditionally.

> We were about five hours out of Frankfurt flying over the North Atlantic, and I was in my crew rest seat, taking my scheduled rest break. All of a sudden the curtains parted violently, and I was told to go to the cockpit, right now, to see the captain. As soon as I got there I noticed that the crew had one of those "all business" looks on their faces. The captain handed me a printed message. I quickly read the message and realized the importance of it. The message was from Atlanta, addressed to our flight, and simply said, "All airways over the Continental U.S. are closed. Land ASAP at the nearest airport, advise your destination."

> Now, when a dispatcher tells you to land immediately without suggesting which airport, one can assume that the dispatcher has reluctantly given up control of the flight to the captain. We knew it was a serious situation and we needed to find terra firma quickly. It was quickly decided that the nearest airport was four hundred miles away, behind our right shoulder, in Gander, on the island of Newfoundland.

> A quick request was made to the Canadian traffic controller and a right turn, directly to Gander, was approved immediately. We found out later why there was no hesitation

by the Canadian controller approving our request. We, the in-flight crew, were told to get the airplane ready for an immediate landing. While this was going on, another message arrived from Atlanta telling us about some terrorist activity in the New York area.

We briefed the in-flight crew about going to Gander and we went about our business "closing down" the airplane for a landing. A few minutes later, I went back to the cockpit to find out that some airplanes had been hijacked and were being flown into buildings all over the U.S. We decided to make an announcement and lie to the passengers for the time being. We told them that an instrument problem had arisen on the airplane and that we needed to land at Gander to have it checked. We promised to give more information after landing in Gander. There were many unhappy passengers, but that is par for the course.

We landed in Gander about forty minutes after the start of this episode. There were already about twenty other airplanes on the ground from all over the world. After we parked on the ramp, the captain made the following announcement. "Ladies and gentlemen, you must be wondering if all these airplanes around us have the same instrument problem we have. But the reality is that we are here for a good reason." Then he went on to explain the little bit we knew about the situation in the U.S. There were loud gasps and stares of disbelief. Local time at Gander was 12:30 p.m. (11:00 a.m. EST) Gander control told us to stay put. No one was allowed to get off the aircraft. No one on the ground was allowed to come near the aircrafts. Only a car from the airport police would come around once in a while, look us over, and go on to the next airplane.

In the next hour or so, all the airways over the North Atlantic were vacated, and Gander alone ended up with fifty-three airplanes from all over the world, out of which twenty-seven were flying U.S. flags. We were told that each and every plane was to be off-loaded, one at a time, with the foreign carriers given the priority. We were number fourteen in the U.S. category. We were further told that we would be given a tentative time to deplane at 6 p.m.

Meanwhile, bits of news started to come in over the aircraft radio, and for the first time we learned that airplanes were flown into the World Trade Center in New York and into the Pentagon in D.C. People were trying to use their cell phones, but were unable to connect due to a different cell system in Canada. Some did get through, but were only able to get to the Canadian operator, who would tell them that the lines to the U.S. were either blocked or jammed and to try again. Some time, late in the evening, the news filtered to us that the World Trade Center buildings had collapsed and that a fourth hijacking had resulted in a crash. Now the passengers were totally bewildered and emotionally exhausted, but stayed calm as we kept reminding them to look around to see that we were not the only ones in this predicament.

There were fifty-two other planes with people on them in the same situation. We also told them that the Canadian government was in charge and we were at their mercy. True to their word, at 6 p.m., Gander airport told us that our turn to deplane would come at 11 a.m., the next morning. That took the last wind out of the passengers, and they simply resigned and accepted this news without much noise and really started to get into a mode of spending the night on the airplane.

Gander had promised us any and all medical attention if needed: medicine, water, and lavatory servicing. And they were true to their word. Fortunately, we had no medical situation during the night. We did have a young lady who was thirty-three weeks into her pregnancy. We took really good care of her. The night passed without any further complications on our airplane despite the uncomfortable sleeping arrangements. About 10:30 on the morning of the twelfth, we were told to get ready to leave the aircraft.

A convoy of school buses showed up at the side of the airplane, the stairway was hooked up, and the passengers were taken to the terminal for "processing." We, the crew, were taken to the same terminal but were told to go to a different section, where we were processed through Immigration and customs and then had to register with the Red Cross. After that we were isolated from our passengers and were taken in a caravan of vans to a very small hotel in the town of Gander. We had no idea where our passengers were going.

The town of Gander has a population of 10,400 people. Red Cross told us that they were going to process about 10,500 passengers from all the airplanes that were forced into Gander. We were told to just relax at the hotel and wait for a call to go back to the airport, but not to expect that call for a while. We found out the total scope of the terror back home only after getting to our hotel and turning on the TV, twenty-four hours after it all started.

Meanwhile, we enjoyed ourselves, going around town discovering things and enjoying the hospitality. The people were so friendly, and they just knew that we were the "Plane People." We all had a great time until we got that call two days later, on the fourteenth at 7 a.m. We made it to the airport by 8:30 a.m. and left for Atlanta at 12:30 p.m., arriving in Atlanta at about 4:30 p.m. (Gander is an hour and thirty minutes ahead of EST—yes, one hour and thirty minutes.)

But that's not what I wanted to tell you. What passengers told us was so uplifting and incredible, and the timing couldn't have been better. We found out that Gander and the surrounding small communities within a seventy-five kilometer radius had closed all the high schools, meeting halls, lodges, and any other large gathering places. They converted all these facilities to mass lodging areas. Some had cots set up; some had mats with sleeping bags and pillows set up. All the high school students had to volunteer taking care of the "guests."

Our 218 passengers ended up in a town called Lewisporte, about forty-five kilometers from Gander. There they were put in a high school. If any women wanted to be in a women-only facility, that was arranged. Families were kept together.

All the elderly passengers were given no choice and were taken to private homes. Remember that young pregnant lady? She was put up in a private home right across the street from a twenty-four-hour urgent care–type facility. There were DDS on call, and they had both male and female nurses available and stayed with the crowd for the duration. Phone calls and e-mails to the U.S. and Europe were available for everyone once a day. During the day the passengers were given a choice of "excursion" trips. Some people went on boat cruises of the lakes and harbors. Some went to see the local forests. Local bakeries stayed open to make fresh bread for the guests. Food was prepared by all the residents and brought to the school for those who elected to stay put.

Others were driven to the eatery of their choice and fed. They were given tokens to go to the local Laundromat to wash their clothes since their luggage was still on the aircraft. In other words, every single need was met for those unfortunate travelers. Passengers were crying while telling us these stories. After all that, they were delivered to the airport right on time and without a single one missing or late. All because the local Red Cross had all the information about the goings-on back at Gander and knew which group needed to leave for the airport at what time. Absolutely incredible.

When passengers came onboard, it was like they had been on a cruise. Everybody knew everybody else by their name. They were swapping stories of their stay, impressing each other with who had the better time. It was mind-boggling. Our flight back to Atlanta looked like a party flight. We simply stayed out of their way. The passengers had totally bonded, and they were calling each other by their first names, exchanging phone numbers, addresses, and e-mail addresses.

And then a strange thing happened. One of our business class passengers approached me and asked if he could speak over the PA to his fellow passengers. We never, never allow that. But something told me to get out of his way. I said, "Of course." The gentleman picked up the PA and reminded everyone about what they had just gone through in the last few days. He reminded them of the hospitality they had received at the hands of total strangers. He further stated that he would like to do something in return for the good folks of the town of Lewisporte. He said he was going to set up a trust fund under the name of DELTA 15 (our flight number). The purpose of the trust fund is to provide a scholarship for high school student(s) of Lewisporte to help them go to college. He asked for donations of any amount from his fellow travelers.

When the paper with donations got back to us with the amounts, names, phone numbers, and addresses, it totaled to $14.5K or about $20K Canadian. The gentleman who started all this turned out to be an MD from Virginia. He promised to match the donations and to start the administrative work on the scholarship. He also said that he would forward this proposal to Delta Corporate and ask them to donate as well.

Why all of this? Just because some people in far away places were kind to some strangers, who happened to literally drop in among them? WHY NOT?

The town of Lewisporte is forty-five minutes away, and the people of that town also fed all passengers three meals a day and provided countless blankets, toothbrushes, and toiletries for passengers on that flight. The Salvation Army of Lewisporte as well as local schools provided housing, showers, and Internet access. These two cities provided the temporarily displaced airline passengers unequaled hospitality and showed them great kindness.

# Principle 17

## The Principle of
## Knowing That God Controls It All

**Haggai 2:8–9**

*The silver is mine and the gold is mine, declares the Lord Almighty.*

Not only is the silver and gold the Lord's—everything belongs to God. So why not give it all to Him? Paul says in 1 Corinthians 4:2 that it is required that those who have been given a trust must prove faithful. A steward is simply a manager of someone else's money and possessions. We give it all back to God and manage it as He would have us to.

**Psalm 50:10**

*For every animal of the forest is mine, and the cattle on a thousand hills.*

A successful businessperson by the name of R. G. LeTourneau was in the business of manufacturing earth-moving equipment. As his business grew and prospered, he decided to increase his tithe over and above the tenth. In time he eventually increased his giving to 90 percent of his income and lived on the rest. Instead of giving the tenth, he lived on the tenth.

God blessed this man bountifully and used his inventive God-given genius and creativity to reach the world for the gospel. While there are many great giving Scriptures in the Bible, none seems more specific than the directive that every person should give what is in his heart, not reluctantly or under compulsion. Mr. LeTourneau certainly recognized the value of 2 Corinthians 9:7 and that it was God who gave him the power to gain wealth.

# Principle 18

## The Principle of
## Knowing the Origin

**1 Chronicles 29:10–12**

*Praise be to you, O Lord, God of our father Israel, from everlasting to everlasting. Yours, O Lord, is the greatness and the power and the glory and the majesty and the splendor, for everything in heaven and earth is yours. Yours, O Lord, is the kingdom; you are exalted as head over all. Wealth and honor come from you; you are the ruler of all things. In your hands are strength and power.*

This Scripture reminds us that wealth and honor come from God. Did you think that maybe it was all because of your education, intelligence, and hard work that you became wealthy? Of course, we do have a stewardship responsibility to work hard and be diligent, but the power to get wealth and to produce wealth comes from Him. Some have not yet learned this lesson, and still others have forgotten it. The bottom line is this: The origin or beginning of all good things comes from their Source—God.

# Principle 19

## The Principle of
## Lacking Absolutely Nothing

**Proverbs 28:27**

*He who gives to the poor will lack nothing, but he who closes his eyes to them receives many curses.*

This is a very strong in-your-face, verse of Scripture, which indicates that if you want to go through life lacking nothing, you had better be giving to the poor. Did you ever wonder what it is really like to be in true poverty? In countries of prosperity, few qualify as poor. While having an adequate income is necessary to sustain oneself, there is much more to a sense of well-being than having a steady income. The good life without poverty includes belonging to a community, having good health, possessing a sense of inner peace, having the freedom of choice, developing an occupational livelihood, working in a healthy environment, and enjoying clean air and pure water.

The World Bank website offers the following quotes from people around the world living in poverty.

• "Poverty is like living in jail, living under bondage, waiting to be free." —Jamaica •

"If you want to do something and have no power to do it, it is talauchi (poverty)." —Nigeria

• "Poverty is lack of freedom, enslaved by crushing daily burden, by depression and fear of what the future will bring." —Georgia

• "Lack of work worries me. My children were hungry and I told them the rice is cooking, until they fell asleep from hunger." —an older man from Bedsa, Egypt

• "A better life for me is to be healthy, peaceful and live in love without hunger. Love is more than anything. Money has no value in the absence of love." —a poor older woman in Ethiopia

• "When one is poor, she has no say in public, she feels inferior. She has no food, so there is famine in her house; no clothing, and no progress in her family." —a woman from Uganda

• "For a poor person everything is terrible—illness, humiliation, shame. We are cripples; we are afraid of everything; we depend on everyone. No one needs us. We are like garbage that everyone wants to get rid of." —a blind woman from Tiraspol, Moldova

• "I repeat that we need water as badly as we need air." —a woman from Tash-Bulak, the Kyrgyz Republic

• "Every day I am afraid of the next." —Russia

• "After one poor crop, we need three good harvests to return to normal." —Vietnam

• "If you don't have money today, your disease will take you to your grave."—an old woman from Ghana

So how is it with you? Do you feel as though you lack something? Try doing what the Bible says to do...give to the poor. If you continue doing so, you will lack absolutely nothing.

# Principle 20

## The Principle of
## Laying Up Treasures

**Timothy 6:19**

*In this way they will lay up treasure for themselves as a firm foundation for the coming age, so that they may take hold of the life that is truly life.*

There is an ancient legend about the monk who found a precious stone, a precious jewel. A short time later, the monk met a traveler who said he was hungry and asked if the monk would share some of his provisions. When the monk opened his bag, the traveler saw the precious stone and, on an impulse, asked the monk if he could have it. Amazingly, the monk gave the traveler the stone.

The traveler departed quickly, overjoyed with his new possession. However, a few days later, he came back, searching for the monk. He returned the stone to the monk and made a request: "Please give me something more valuable, more precious than this stone. Please give me that which enabled you to give me this precious stone!"2

Jesus teaches us that the world in itself is not important, but how we exist in it and where it leads us is the important consideration. This world is not an end to itself, but a stage along the way.

Since this world is not the end of our path, we should never sell out to it, lose our hearts to it, or lose our souls because of it. Richard

Glover, in his Commentary on Matthew, says this: "He builds too low who builds beneath the skies."

# Principle 21

## The Principle of
## Learning Real Success

**Joshua 1:8–9**

*Do not let this Book of the Law depart from your mouth;
meditate on it day and night, so that you may be careful
to do everything written in it. Then you will be prosperous and successful.*

Becoming prosperous and successful is a direct result of obedience. In this Scripture, God challenges us to meditate upon the
Word. The emphasis placed here is not upon education, knowledge,
or experience. It is upon obedience. It is one thing to understand and
quite another to walk in obedience.

Study the life of Joshua if you desire success. Some 1300 years
before Christ, Joshua was born into a family of Egyptian slavery.
Growing up under Egyptian rule he experienced firsthand both the
plagues of Egypt and the exodus miracle. Arriving at the border of
the Promised Land under the great leadership of Moses, he was one
of twelve spies that were sent out to scout the land. Only Joshua and
Caleb returned with a faith-filled report.

After the death of the prophet Moses, the Lord chose Joshua to
get the people ready to cross over into the land of promise. His entire
life was one of obedience and faith. When we obey God's principles

of provision, He will see to it that we also benefit from biblical principles resulting in prosperity and success.

# Principle 22

## The Principle of
## Lending to the Lord

**Proverbs 19:17**

> *He who is kind to the poor lends to the Lord, and he*
> *will reward him for what he has done.*

In America, and many other nations all around the world, this generation has access to untold quantities of wealth. Yet even though our wealth and blessing have increased, still the need to give money to the poor and food to the hungry has never been greater than right now. Untold millions are needed to reach the world with the gospel. Our first priority is to read, know, and obey the Word of God.

The following story is told by Louis Lehman in the March 1999 edition of *Guideposts*:

> When I was growing up, my father used to say, "No matter who they are or what they do, treat your neighbors with love." I didn't fully understand what he meant until on Sunday on our way to church, when we spotted someone shoveling corn from our crib into a battered old truck. Dad stopped the car and got out. The man looked up and froze. I knew this man. Everybody in town suspected him of stealing their gas! No one had ever confronted him for fear of his violent temper. Now we'd caught him red-handed.

What was Dad going to do? "If that's not enough," my father said evenly, "come back tomorrow. Take as much as you need. Remember, you're my neighbor." The man dropped his shovel and hung his head. He never stole from us or anyone else in town again, as far as I know. Perhaps he learned how to be a good neighbor that day. I know I did.

How would you have reacted? What would you have done if someone in need stole from you? If we are kind to the poor, Scripture promises us that in doing so we are lending to the Lord. Lending to the Lord brings great reward both in this life and the life to come.

# Principle 23

## The Principle of
## Putting Your Needs Last

**1 Kings 17:9–16**

*Go at once to Zarephath of Sidon and stay there. I have commanded a widow in that place to supply you with food. So he went to Zarephath. When he came to the town gate, a widow was there gathering sticks. He called to her and asked, "Would you bring me a little water in a jar so I may have a drink?" As she was going to get it, he called, "And bring me, please, a piece of bread."*

*"As surely as the Lord your God lives," she replied, "I don't have any bread-only a handful of flour in a jar and a little oil in a jug. I am gathering a few sticks to take home and make a meal for myself and my son, that we may eat it—and die."*

*Elijah said to her, "Don't be afraid. Go home and do as you have said. But first make a small cake of bread for me from what you have and bring it to me, and then make something for yourself and your son. For this is what the Lord, the God of Israel, says: 'The jar of flour will not be used up and the jug of oil will not run dry until the day the Lord gives rain on the land.'" She went away and did as Elijah had told her. So there was food every day for Elijah and for the woman and her family. For the jar of flour was not used up and the jug of oil did not run dry, in keeping with the word of the Lord spoken by Elijah.*

Here is the account of a great lady who placed her own personal needs last, even to the point of giving away her last meal to a stranger. She was a Phoenician women who lived on the Mediterranean coast, living a very simple life, her needs being met one day at a time. She had a willingness to obey and did so by showing kindness to Elijah. She was a woman of hospitality and a model for all of us.

Placing the needs of others ahead of her own, she gave all she had to serve this man of God. Even though she truly believed that she was about to prepare the last meal for herself and her son and then die, still she honored Elijah's request to be fed first. This was no easy decision. What would you have done given the same circumstance? What areas have you been stretched in and called upon to exercise both obedience and faith? Because she placed her needs last and the plight of others first, God blessed her beyond her need and expectation.

# Principle 24

## The Principle of
## Plenty Left Over

**2 Corinthians 9:8–9**

*God is able to make it up to you by giving you everything you need and more so that there will not only be enough for your own needs but plenty left over to give joyfully to others. (rsv)*

It's not about God making you rich just because you tithe regularly. However, God has promised to meet your needs. That promise may come by way of a job so that you can work hard and provide for your family. When you give, it is with complete confidence that God is faithful to His Word. You can trust Him to take care of you. You can trust Him with your whole heart and your whole mind; you can trust Him with your life.

Some of us find it easier to trust God for eternity than for today's bills and tomorrow's problems. When it comes to giving, we must do so in complete confidence that our God will not only meet our needs, but allow us to have plenty left over so that we can joyfully share it with others.

# Principle 25

## The Principle of
## Refreshing Others and Being Refreshed

**Proverbs 11:25**

*A generous man will prosper; he who refreshes others will himself be refreshed.*

In England, the story is told, a lady opened her front door in a driving rainstorm. A rain soaked lady stood there and said, "Pardon, the wind and rain have completely done me in and I forgot to take an umbrella. I was wondering if I might borrow one—I'll return it of course tomorrow." *Now who is this stranger that stands and asks of me?*, the lady of the house thought. *How do I know she'd bring it back?* The lady had an older umbrella behind the door with broken spines. *Even if the visitor doesn't return it*, she said to herself, *I wouldn't have lost much.* So she handed it to the stranger. The next day a fine carriage approached the house and stopped in front of her house. A footman came up to the door and politely knocked. "Pardon madam. The Queen wishes to express her thanks for your kindness of yesterday," he said as he handed her the borrowed umbrella. *Oh*, she thought. *Here was the Queen, and I gave her less than the best I had.*

What is the value of your gift? Whom have you refreshed lately?

# Principle 26

## The Principle of
## Sharing Your Blessing

**1 Timothy 6:18**

*Command them to do good, to be rich in good deeds, and to be generous and willing to share.*

**Luke 3:11**

*He answereth and saith unto them, He that hath two coats, let him impart to him that hath none; and he that hath meat, let him do likewise. (kjv)*

**Matthew 14:15–21**

*As evening approached, the disciples came to him and said, "This is a remote place, and it's already getting late. Send the crowds away, so they can go to the villages and buy themselves some food." Jesus replied, "They do not need to go away. You give them something to eat." "We have here only five loaves of bread and two fish," they answered. "Bring them here to me," he said. And he directed the people to sit down on the grass. Taking the five loaves and the two fish and looking up to heaven, he gave thanks and broke the loaves. Then he gave them to the disciples, and the disciples gave them to the people. They all ate and were satisfied, and the disciples picked up twelve basketfuls of broken pieces that were left over. The number of those who ate was about five thousand men, besides women and children.*

This is the story of the feeding of the five thousand. Jesus and His disciples were tired, and He suggested they get off by themselves and rest a while. But as they went, the people saw them and came in great numbers. No doubt the word quickly spread around into the surrounding towns, and a crowd of five thousand people gathered. When Jesus saw them, He was "moved with compassion." He saw their needs and was concerned to help them.

Being captivated by the teaching of Jesus, the time passed very quickly. In this story of the feeding of the five thousand, when the multitude grew hungry, all the disciples could think of was to "send them away." After all, there were five thousand of them, and the disciples had no food or money. One thing the disciples overlooked. They were correct in feeling they were up against a great need, but they failed to consider their own resources, and they also failed to consider the power of God. There is never a situation that we and God together cannot handle.

In the face of that hungry multitude, it never occurred to Christ to "send them away." John tells us, "He Himself knew what He would do." God always has a plan to meet every situation. No emergency ever takes God by surprise. Jesus asked the disciples, "How many loaves have you?" Andrew said, "There is a lad here with five barley loaves and two small fishes." Long story short, the young boy gladly offered up his lunch and shared all he had with Jesus. Jesus multiplied it, and because of one small boy's willingness to share, the entire crowd was fed with plenty left over.

# Principle 27

## The Principle of
## The Ultimate Gift

**John 3:16**

*For God so loved the world, that he gave his only begotten Son, that whosoever believeth in him should not perish, but have everlasting life. (kjv)*

**Romans 8:31–33**

*He who did not spare his own Son, but gave him up for us all—how will he not also, along with him, graciously give us all things?*

Sometimes our immaturity as Christians shows when we stay in the "asking/demanding" mode and forget to offer thanks for all that Christ has given us. Not only are we blessed daily with His benefits, but let us not forget the "ultimate" gift He gave us—His life.

This thought is illustrated by the story of a small boy.

A little boy came into the kitchen one evening while his mom was fixing supper. He handed her a piece of paper he'd been writing on. So after wiping her hands on her apron, she read it, and this is what it said:

- For mowing the grass, $5.00.
- For making my own bed this week, $1.00.
- For going to the store, $0.50.
- For playing with baby brother while you went shopping, $0.25.
- For taking out the trash, $1.00.
- For getting a good report card, $5.00.
- And for raking the yard, $2.00.

Well, she looked at him standing there expectantly, and a thousand memories flashed through her mind. So she picked up the paper and, turning it over, this is what she wrote:

- For the nine months I carried you, growing inside me, No Charge,
- For the nights I sat up with you, doctored you, prayed for you, No Charge.
- For the time and the tears and the cost through the years, No Charge.
- For the nights filled with dread and the worries ahead, there's No Charge.
- For advice and the knowledge and the cost of your college, No Charge.
- For the toys, food, and clothes and for wiping your nose, there's No Charge, Son.
- When you add it all up, the full cost of my love is No Charge.

Well, when he finished reading, he had great big tears in his eyes.

And he looked up at her and said, "Mama, I sure do love you."

Then he took the pen and in great big letters he wrote, PAID IN FULL.

What are you expecting from God in addition to the price He has already paid?

# Summary

**2 Corinthians 9:8**

*And God is able to provide you with every blessing in abundance, so that you may always have enough of everything and may provide in abundance for every good work. (rsv)*

In summary, here is why God allows many to become prosperous: You are blessed or will be blessed so that you can be a blessing to others. God does not prosper you for the purpose of raising your standard of living; He prospers you so that you can raise your standard of giving.

Nothing happens in the economy of God until you give something away. It is a universal law of God. Paul very appropriately reminds us: "Remember this: Whoever sows sparingly will also reap sparingly, and whoever sows generously will also reap generously" (2 Corinthians 9:6).

Giving is the trigger for God's financial miracles. When you give to the Kingdom of God, it will be given back to you. But where will it come from? Who will give to you? Will God cause money to float down from heaven so that your needs are met? No. The Bible says, "Shall men give into your...[life]" (Luke 6:38, kjv). This is how the cycle of blessing works. When you give to God, He in turn causes others to give to you.

# Scriptures on Wealth, Riches and Prosperity

## Wealth

**Genesis 31:1**

*Jacob Flees from Laban: Now Jacob heard the words of Laban's sons, saying, "Jacob has taken away all that was our father's, and from what was our father's he has acquired all this wealth." (nkjv)*

**Genesis 34:29**

*And all their wealth: All their little ones and their wives they took captive; and they plundered even all that was in the houses. (nkjv)*

**Deuteronomy 8:17**

*Then you say in your heart, "My power and the might of my hand have gained me this wealth." (nkjv)*

**Deuteronomy 8:18**

*And you shall remember the Lord your God, for it is He who gives you power to get wealth, that He may estab-*

*lish His covenant which He swore to your fathers, as it is this day. (nkjv)*

## Ruth 2:1

*Ruth Meets Boaz: There was a relative of Naomi's husband, a man of great wealth, of the family of Elimelech. His name was Boaz. (nkjv)*

## 1 Kings 10:14

*Solomon's Great Wealth: The weight of gold that came to Solomon yearly was six hundred and sixty-six talents of gold. (nkjv)*

## 2 Kings 15:20

*And Menahem exacted the money from Israel, from all the very wealthy, from each man fifty shekels of silver, to give to the king of Assyria. So the king of Assyria turned back, and did not stay there in the land. (nkjv)*

## 2 Chronicles 1:11

*Then God said to Solomon: "Because this was in your heart, and you have not asked riches or wealth or honor or the life of your enemies, nor have you asked long life—but have asked wisdom and knowledge for yourself, that you may judge My people over whom I have made you king." (nkjv)*

**2 Chronicles 1:12**

*Wisdom and knowledge are granted to you; and I will give you riches and wealth and honor, such as none of the kings have had who were before you, nor shall any after you have the like. (nkjv)*

**2 Chronicles 9:13**

*Solomon's Great Wealth (see also 1 Kings 10:14–29; 2 Chronicles 1:14–17): The weight of gold that came to Solomon yearly was six hundred and sixty-six talents of gold. (nkjv)*

**2 Chronicles 32:27**

*Hezekiah's Wealth and Honor (see also 2 Kings 20:12–21; Isaiah 39:1): Hezekiah had very great riches and honor. And he made himself treasuries for silver, for gold, for precious stones, for spices, for shields, and for all kinds of desirable items. (nkjv)*

**Job 6:22**

*Did I ever say, "Bring something to me"? Or, "Offer a bribe for me from your wealth"? (nkjv)*

**Job 15:29**

*He will not be rich, nor will his wealth continue, nor will his possessions overspread the earth. (nkjv)*

### Job 20:10

*His children will seek the favor of the poor, And his hands will restore his wealth. (nkjv)*

### Job 21:13

*They spend their days in wealth, And in a moment go down to the grave. (nkjv)*

### Job 30:1

*Job's Wealth Now Poverty: But now they mock at me, men younger than I, whose fathers I disdained to put with the dogs of my flock. (nkjv)*

### Job 31:25

*If I have rejoiced because my wealth was great, and because my hand had gained much. (nkjv)*

### Psalm 49:6

*Those who trust in their wealth, and boast in the multitude of their riches. (nkjv)*

**Psalm 49:10**

*For he sees wise men die; likewise the fool and the senseless person perish, and leave their wealth to others. (nkjv)*

**Psalm 112:3**

*Wealth and riches will be in his house, and his righteousness endures forever. (nkjv)*

**Proverbs 5:10**

*Lest aliens be filled with your wealth, and your labors go to the house of a foreigner. (nkjv)*

**Proverbs 8:21**

*That I may cause those who love me to inherit wealth, that I may fill their treasuries. (nkjv)*

**Proverbs 10:15**

*The rich man's wealth is his strong city; the destruction of the poor is their poverty. (nkjv)*

**Proverbs 13:11**

*Wealth gained by dishonesty will be diminished, but he who gathers by labor will increase. (nkjv)*

### Proverbs 13:22

*A good man leaves an inheritance to his children's children, but the wealth of the sinner is stored up for the righteous. (nkjv)*

### Proverbs 18:11

*The rich man's wealth is his strong city, and like a high wall in his own esteem. (nkjv)*

### Proverbs 19:4

*Wealth makes many friends, but the poor is separated from his friend. (nkjv)*

### Proverbs 29:3

*Whoever loves wisdom makes his father rejoice, but a companion of harlots wastes his wealth. (nkjv)*

### Ecclesiastes 5:19

*As for every man to whom God has given riches and wealth, and given him power to eat of it, to receive his heritage and rejoice in his labor—this is the gift of God. (nkjv)*

**Ecclesiastes 6:1**

*Wealth Is Not the Goal of Life: There is an evil which I have seen under the sun, and it is common among men. (nkjv)*

**Ecclesiastes 6:2**

*A man to whom God has given riches and wealth and honor, so that he lacks nothing for himself of all he desires; yet God does not give him power to eat of it, but a foreigner consumes it. This is vanity, and it is an evil affliction. (nkjv)*

**Song of Solomon 8:7**

*Many waters cannot quench love, nor can the floods drown it. If a man would give for love, all the wealth of his house, it would be utterly despised. (nkjv)*

**Isaiah 60:5**

*Then you shall see and become radiant, and your heart shall swell with joy; because the abundance of the sea shall be turned to you, the wealth of the Gentiles shall come to you. (nkjv)*

**Isaiah 60:11**

*Therefore your gates shall be open continually; they shall not be shut day or night, that men may bring to you the*

*wealth of the Gentiles, and their kings in procession.
(nkjv)*

## Jeremiah 15:13

*Your wealth and your treasures, I will give as plunder
without price, because of all your sins, throughout your
territories. (nkjv)*

## Jeremiah 17:3

*O My mountain in the field, I will give as plunder your
wealth, all your treasures, and your high places of sin
within all your borders. (nkjv)*

## Jeremiah 20:5

*Moreover I will deliver all the wealth of this city, all
its produce, and all its precious things; all the treasures
of the kings of Judah I will give into the hand of their
enemies, who will plunder them, seize them, and carry
them to Babylon. (nkjv)*

## Ezekiel 29:19

*Therefore thus says the Lord God: "Surely I will give
the land of Egypt to Nebuchadnezzar king of Babylon;
he shall take away her wealth, carry off her spoil, and
remove her pillage; and that will be the wages for his
army." (nkjv)*

**Ezekiel 30:4**

*The sword shall come upon Egypt, and great anguish shall be in Ethiopia, when the slain fall in Egypt, and they take away her wealth, and her foundations are broken down. (nkjv)*

**Hosea 12:8**

*And Ephraim said, "Surely I have become rich, I have found wealth for myself; In all my labors, they shall find in me no iniquity that is sin." (nkjv)*

**Nahum 2:9**

*Take spoil of silver! Take spoil of gold! There is no end of treasure, or wealth of every desirable prize. (nkjv)*

**Zechariah 14:14**

*Judah also will fight at Jerusalem. And the wealth of all the surrounding nations shall be gathered together: Gold, silver, and apparel in great abundance. (nkjv)*

**Revelation 3:17**

*Because you say, "I am rich, have become wealthy, and have need of nothing"—and do not know that you are wretched, miserable, poor, blind, and naked. (nkjv)*

**Revelation 18:19**

*They threw dust on their heads and cried out, weeping and wailing, and saying, "Alas, alas, that great city, in which all who had ships on the sea became rich by her wealth! For in one hour she is made desolate." (nkjv)*

## Rich and Riches

**Genesis 13:2**

*Abram was very rich in livestock, in silver, and in gold. (nkjv)*

**Genesis 14:23**

*That I will take nothing, from a thread to a sandal strap, and that I will not take anything that is yours, lest you should say, "I have made Abram rich." (nkjv)*

**Genesis 49:20**

*Bread from Asher shall be rich, and he shall yield royal dainties. (nkjv)*

**Exodus 30:15**

*The rich shall not give more and the poor shall not give less than half a shekel, when you give an offering to the Lord, to make atonement for yourselves. (nkjv)*

**Leviticus 25:47**

*Now if a sojourner or stranger close to you becomes rich, and one of your brethren who dwells by him becomes poor, and sells himself to the stranger or sojourner close to you, or to a member of the stranger's family. (nkjv)*

**Numbers 13:20**

*Whether the land is rich or poor; and whether there are forests there or not. Be of good courage. And bring some of the fruit of the land. (nkjv)*

**Ruth 3:10**

*Then he said, "Blessed are you of the Lord, my daughter! For you have shown more kindness at the end than at the beginning, in that you did not go after young men, whether poor or rich." (nkjv)*

**1 Samuel 2:7**

*The Lord makes poor and makes rich; He brings low and lifts up. (nkjv)*

**1 Samuel 25:2**

*Now there was a man in Maon whose business was in Carmel, and the man was very rich. He had three thousand sheep and a thousand goats. And he was shearing his sheep in Carmel. (nkjv)*

**2 Samuel 12:1**

*Then the Lord sent Nathan to David. And he came to him, and said to him: "There were two men in one city, one rich and the other poor." (nkjv)*

**2 Samuel 12:2**

*The rich man had exceedingly many flocks and herds. (nkjv)*

**2 Samuel 12:4**

*And a traveler came to the rich man, who refused to take from his own flock and from his own herd to prepare one for the wayfaring man who had come to him; but he took the poor man's lamb and prepared it for the man who had come to him. (nkjv)*

**2 Samuel 19:32**

*Now Barzillai was a very aged man, eighty years old. And he had provided the king with supplies while he stayed at Mahanaim, for he was a very rich man. (nkjv)*

**1 Chronicles 4:40**

*And they found rich, good pasture, and the land was broad, quiet, and peaceful; for some Hamites formerly lived there. (nkjv)*

**Nehemiah 9:25**

*And they took strong cities and a rich land, and possessed houses full of all goods, cisterns already dug, vineyards, olive groves, and fruit trees in abundance. So they ate and were filled and grew fat,*

*And delighted themselves in your great goodness. (nkjv)*

**Nehemiah 9:35**

*For they have not served You in their kingdom, or in the many good things that you gave them, or in the large and rich land which You set before them; nor did they turn from their wicked works. (nkjv)*

**Job 15:29**

*He will not be rich, nor will his wealth continue, nor will his possessions overspread the earth. (nkjv)*

**Job 27:19**

*The rich man will lie down, but not be gathered up; he opens his eyes, and he is no more. (nkjv)*

**Job 34:19**

*Yet He is not partial to princes, nor does He regard the rich more than the poor; for they are all the work of His hands. (nkjv)*

**Psalm 45:12**

*And the daughter of Tyre will come with a gift; the rich among the people will seek your favor. (nkjv)*

**Psalm 49:2**

*Both low and high, rich and poor together. (nkjv)*

**Psalm 49:16**

*Do not be afraid when one becomes rich, when the glory of his house is increased. (nkjv)*

**Psalm 66:12**

*You have caused men to ride over our heads; we went through fire and through water; but You brought us out to rich fulfillment. (nkjv)*

**Proverbs 10:4**

*He who has a slack hand becomes poor, but the hand of the diligent makes rich. (nkjv)*

**Proverbs 10:22**

*The blessing of the Lord makes one rich, and He adds no sorrow with it. (nkjv)*

**Proverbs 11:25**

*The generous soul will be made rich, and he who waters will also be watered himself. (nkjv)*

**Proverbs 13:4**

*The soul of a lazy man desires, and has nothing; but the soul of the diligent shall be made rich. (nkjv)*

**Proverbs 13:7**

*There is one who makes himself rich, yet has nothing; and one who makes himself poor, yet has great riches. (nkjv)*

**Proverbs 14:20**

*The poor man is hated even by his own neighbor, but the rich has many friends. (nkjv)*

**Proverbs 18:23**

*The poor man uses entreaties, but the rich answers roughly. (nkjv)*

**Proverbs 21:17**

*He who loves pleasure will be a poor man; he who loves wine and oil will not be rich. (nkjv)*

### Proverbs 22:2

*The rich and the poor have this in common, the Lord is the maker of them all. (nkjv)*

### Proverbs 22:7

*The rich rules over the poor, and the borrower is servant to the lender. (nkjv)*

### Proverbs 22:16

*He who oppresses the poor to increase his riches, and he who gives to the rich, will surely come to poverty. (nkjv)*

### Colossians 1:27

*To them God willed to make known what are the riches of the glory of this mystery among the Gentiles: which is Christ in you, the hope of glory. (nkjv)*

### Colossians 2:2

*That their hearts may be encouraged, being knit together in love, and attaining to all riches of the full assurance of understanding, to the knowledge of the mystery of God, both of the Father and of Christ. (nkjv)*

**1 Timothy 6:17**

*Command those who are rich in this present age not to be haughty, nor to trust in uncertain riches but in the living God, who gives us richly all things to enjoy. (nkjv)*

**Hebrews 11:26**

*Esteeming the reproach of Christ greater riches than the treasures in Egypt; for he looked to the reward. (nkjv)*

**James 5:2**

*Your riches are corrupted, and your garments are moth-eaten. (nkjv)*

**Revelation 5:12**

*Saying with a loud voice: "Worthy is the Lamb who was slain To receive power and riches and wisdom, And strength and honor and glory and blessing!" (nkjv)*

**Revelation 18:17**

*"For in one hour such great riches came to nothing." Every shipmaster, all who travel by ship, sailors, and as many as trade on the sea, stood at a distance. (nkjv)*

# Prosperity

### Deuteronomy 23:5–6

*You shall not seek their peace nor their prosperity all your days forever.*

### 1 Samuel 25:5–6

*And thus you shall say to him who lives in prosperity: "Peace be to you, peace to your house, and peace to all that you have!"*

### 1 Kings 10:7

*However I did not believe the words until I came and saw with my own eyes; and indeed the half was not told me. Your wisdom and prosperity exceed the fame of which I heard.*

### Ezra 9:12–13

*Now therefore, do not give your daughters as wives for their sons, nor take their daughters to your sons; and never seek their peace or prosperity, that you may be strong and eat the good of the land, and leave it as an inheritance to your children forever.*

**Job 15:21**

*Dreadful sounds are in his ears; In prosperity the destroyer comes upon him.*

**Job 21:16**

*Indeed their prosperity is not in their hand; the counsel of the wicked is far from me.*

**Job 30:15**

*Terrors are turned upon me; They pursue my honor as the wind, And my prosperity has passed like a cloud.*

**Job 36:11–12**

*If they obey and serve Him, they shall spend their days in prosperity, and their years in pleasures. But if they do not obey, they shall perish by the sword, and they shall die without knowledge.*

**Psalm 25:13**

*He himself shall dwell in prosperity, and his descendants shall inherit the earth.*

### Psalm 30:6–7

*Now in my prosperity I said, "I shall never be moved." Lord, by Your favor You have made my mountain stand strong; You hid Your face, and I was troubled.*

### Psalm 35:27

*Let them shout for joy and be glad, Who favor my righteous cause; And let them say continually, "Let the Lord be magnified, Who has pleasure in the prosperity of His servant."*

### Psalm 68:6

*God sets the solitary in families; He brings out those who are bound into prosperity; But the rebellious dwell in a dry land.*

### Psalm 73:3

*For I was envious of the boastful, when I saw the prosperity of the wicked.*

### Psalm 118:25

*Save now, I pray, O Lord; O Lord, I pray, send now prosperity.*

**Psalm 122:7**

*Peace be within your walls, Prosperity within your palaces.*

**Ecclesiastes 7:14**

*In the day of prosperity be joyful, But in the day of adversity consider: Surely God has appointed the one as well as the other, So that man can find out nothing that will come after him.*

**Jeremiah 22:21**

*I spoke to you in your prosperity, But you said, "I will not hear." This has been your manner from your youth, That you did not obey My voice.*

**Jeremiah 33:9**

*Then it shall be to Me a name of joy, a praise, and an honor before all nations of the earth, who shall hear all the good that I do to them; they shall fear and tremble for all the goodness and all the prosperity that I provide for it.*

**Lamentations 3:17–18**

*You have moved my soul far from peace; I have forgotten prosperity. And I said, "My strength and my hope have perished from the Lord."*

### Daniel 4:27

*Therefore, O king, let my advice be acceptable to you; break off your sins by being righteous, and your iniquities by showing mercy to the poor. Perhaps there may be a lengthening of your prosperity.*

### Daniel 8:25

*Through his cunning He shall cause deceit to prosper under his rule; And he shall exalt himself in his heart. He shall destroy many in their prosperity. He shall even rise against the Prince of princes; But he shall be broken without human means.*

### Zechariah 1:17

*Again proclaim, saying, "Thus says the Lord of hosts: 'My cities shall again spread out through prosperity; The Lord will again comfort Zion, And will again choose Jerusalem.'"*

### Acts 19:25

*He called them together with the workers of similar occupation, and said: "Men, you know that we have our prosperity by this trade."*

### Acts 24:2–4

*And when he was called upon, Tertullus began his accusation, saying: "Seeing that through you we enjoy great peace, and prosperity is being brought to this nation by your foresight, we accept it always and in all places, most noble Felix, with all thankfulness."*

## Prosperous

**Genesis 24:2**

*And the man, wondering at her, remained silent so as to know whether the Lord had made his journey prosperous or not. (nkjv)*

**Genesis 26:13**

*The man began to prosper, and continued prospering until he became very prosperous. (nkjv)*

**Genesis 30:4**

*Thus the man became exceedingly prosperous, and had large flocks, female and male servants, and camels and donkeys. (nkjv)*

**Joshua 1:8**

*This Book of the Law shall not depart from your mouth, but you shall meditate in it day and night, that you may observe to do according to all that is written in it. For then you will make your way prosperous, and then you will have good success. (nkjv)*

### Judges 18:5

*So they said to him, "Please inquire of God, that we may know whether the journey on which we go will be prosperous." (nkjv)*

### Psalm 22:29

*All the prosperous of the earth shall eat and worship; all those who go down to the dust shall bow before Him, even he who cannot keep himself alive. (nkjv)*

### Zechariah 7:7

*Should you not have obeyed the words which the Lord proclaimed through the former prophets when Jerusalem and the cities around it were inhabited and prosperous, and the South and the Lowland were inhabited? (nkjv)*

### Zechariah 8:12

*For the seed shall be prosperous, the vine shall give its fruit, the ground shall give her increase, and the heavens shall give their dew—I will cause the remnant of this people to possess all these. (nkjv)*

# Prosper

**Genesis 24:40**

*But he said to me, "The Lord, before whom I walk, will send His angel with you and prosper your way; and you shall take a wife for my son from my family and from my father's house." (nkjv)*

**Genesis 24:42**

*And this day I came to the well and said, "O Lord God of my master Abraham, if you will now prosper the way in which I go." (nkjv)*

**Genesis 26:13**

*The man began to prosper, and continued prospering until he became very prosperous. (nkjv)*

**Genesis 39:3**

*And his master saw that the Lord was with him and that the Lord made all he did to prosper in his hand. (nkjv)*

**Genesis 39:23**

*The keeper of the prison did not look into anything that was under Joseph's authority, because the Lord was with him; and whatever he did, the Lord made it prosper. (nkjv)*

## Deuteronomy 28:29

*And you shall grope at noonday, as a blind man gropes in darkness; you shall not prosper in your ways; you shall be only oppressed and plundered continually, and no one shall save you. (nkjv)*

## Deuteronomy 29:9

*Therefore keep the words of this covenant, and do them, that you may prosper in all that you do. (nkjv)*

## Deuteronomy 30:5

*Then the Lord your God will bring you to the land which your fathers possessed, and you shall possess it. He will prosper you and multiply you more than your fathers. (nkjv)*

## Joshua 1:7

*Only be strong and very courageous, that you may observe to do according to all the law which Moses My servant commanded you; do not turn from it to the right hand or to the left, that you may prosper wherever you go. (nkjv)*

**Ruth 4:11**

*And all the people who were at the gate, and the elders, said, "We are witnesses. The Lord make the woman who is coming to your house like Rachel and Leah, the two who built the house of Israel; and may you prosper in Ephrathah and be famous in Bethlehem." (nkjv)*

**1 Kings 2:3**

*And keep the charge of the Lord your God: to walk in His ways, to keep His statutes, His commandments, His judgments, and His testimonies, as it is written in the Law of Moses, that you may prosper in all that you do and wherever you turn. (nkjv)*

**1 Kings 22:12**

*And all the prophets prophesied so, saying, "Go up to Ramoth Gilead and prosper, for the Lord will deliver it into the king's hand." (nkjv)*

**1 Kings 22:15**

*Then he came to the king; and the king said to him, "Micaiah, shall we go to war against Ramoth Gilead, or shall we refrain?" And he answered him, "Go and prosper, for the Lord will deliver it into the hand of the king!" (nkjv)*

### 1 Chronicles 22:11

*Now, my son, may the Lord be with you; and may you prosper, and build the house of the Lord your God, as He has said to you. (nkjv)*

### 1 Chronicles 22:13

*Then you will prosper, if you take care to fulfill the statutes and judgments with which the Lord charged Moses concerning Israel. Be strong and of good courage; do not fear nor be dismayed. (nkjv)*

### 2 Chronicles 13:12

*Now look, God Himself is with us as our head, and His priests with sounding trumpets to sound the alarm against you. O children of Israel, do not fight against the Lord God of your fathers, for you shall not prosper! (nkjv)*

### 2 Chronicles 18:11

*And all the prophets prophesied so, saying, "Go up to Ramoth Gilead and prosper, for the Lord will deliver it into the king's hand." (nkjv)*

### 2 Chronicles 18:14

*Then he came to the king; and the king said to him, "Micaiah, shall we go to war against Ramoth Gilead, or shall I refrain?" And he said, "Go and prosper, and they shall be delivered into your hand!" (nkjv)*

## 2 Chronicles 20:20

*So they rose early in the morning and went out into the Wilderness of Tekoa; and as they went out, Jehoshaphat stood and said, "Hear me, O Judah and you inhabitants of Jerusalem: Believe in the Lord your God, and you shall be established; believe His prophets, and you shall prosper." (nkjv)*

## 2 Chronicles 24:20

*Then the Spirit of God came upon Zechariah the son of Jehoiada the priest, who stood above the people, and said to them, "Thus says God: 'Why do you transgress the commandments of the Lord, so that you cannot prosper? Because you have forsaken the Lord, He also has forsaken you.'" (nkjv)*

## 2 Chronicles 26:5

*He sought God in the days of Zechariah, who had understanding in the visions of God; and as long as he sought the Lord, God made him prosper. (nkjv)*

## Nehemiah 1:11

*"O Lord, I pray, please let Your ear be attentive to the prayer of Your servant, and to the prayer of Your servants*

*who desire to fear Your name; and let Your servant pros-
per this day, I pray, and grant him mercy in the sight of
this man." For I was the king's cupbearer. (nkjv)*

## Nehemiah 2:20

*So I answered them, and said to them, "The God of
heaven Himself will prosper us; therefore we His servants will arise and build, but you have no heritage or
right or memorial in Jerusalem." (nkjv)*

## Job 8:6

*If you were pure and upright, surely now He would
awake for you, and prosper your rightful dwelling place.
(nkjv)*

## Job 12:6

*The tents of robbers prosper, and those who provoke God
are secure—in what God provides by His hand. (nkjv)*

## Psalm 1:3

*He shall be like a tree planted by the rivers of water,
that brings forth its fruit in its season, whose leaf also
shall not wither; and whatever he does shall prosper.
(nkjv)*

**Psalm 122:6**

*Pray for the peace of Jerusalem: May they prosper who love you. (nkjv)*

**Proverbs 28:13**

*He who covers his sins will not prosper, but whoever confesses and forsakes them will have mercy. (nkjv)*

**Ecclesiastes 11:6**

*In the morning sow your seed, and in the evening do not withhold your hand; for you do not know which will prosper, either this or that, or whether both alike will be good. (nkjv)*

**Isaiah 48:15**

*I, even I, have spoken; yes, I have called him, I have brought him, and his way will prosper. (nkjv)*

**Isaiah 53:10**

*Yet it pleased the Lord to bruise Him; he has put Him to grief. When You make His soul an offering for sin, he shall see His seed, He shall prolong His days, and the pleasure of the Lord shall prosper in His hand. (nkjv)*

### Isaiah 54:17

*"No weapon formed against you shall prosper, and every tongue which rises against you in judgment you shall condemn. This is the heritage of the servants of the Lord, and their righteousness is from Me," says the Lord. (nkjv)*

### Isaiah 55:11

*So shall My word be that goes forth from My mouth; it shall not return to Me void, but it shall accomplish what I please, and it shall prosper in the thing for which I sent it. (nkjv)*

### Jeremiah 2:37

*Indeed you will go forth from him with your hands on your head; for the Lord has rejected your trusted allies, and you will not prosper by them. (nkjv)*

### Jeremiah 5:28

*They have grown fat, they are sleek; yes, they surpass the deeds of the wicked; they do not plead the cause, the cause of the fatherless; yet they prosper, and the right of the needy they do not defend. (nkjv)*

**Jeremiah 10:21**

*For the shepherds have become dull-hearted, and have not sought the Lord; therefore they shall not prosper, and all their flocks shall be scattered. (nkjv)*

**Jeremiah 12:1**

*Righteous are You, O Lord, when I plead with You; yet let me talk with You about Your judgments. Why does the way of the wicked prosper? Why are those happy who deal so treacherously? (nkjv)*

**Jeremiah 20:11**

*But the Lord is with me as a mighty, awesome One. Therefore my persecutors will stumble, and will not prevail. They will be greatly ashamed, for they will not prosper. Their everlasting confusion will never be forgotten. (nkjv)*

**Jeremiah 22:30**

*Thus says the Lord: "Write this man down as childless, a man who shall not prosper in his days; for none of his descendants shall prosper, sitting on the throne of David, and ruling anymore in Judah." (nkjv)*

### Jeremiah 23:5–6

*"Behold, the days are coming," says the Lord, "That I will raise to David a Branch of righteousness; a King shall reign and prosper, and execute judgment and righteousness in the earth. In His days Judah will be saved, and Israel will dwell safely; now this is His name by which He will be called: THE LORD OUR RIGHTEOUSNESS." (nkjv)*

### Lamentations 1:5

*Her adversaries have become the master, her enemies prosper; for the lord has afflicted her because of the multitude of her transgressions. Her children have gone into captivity before the enemy. (nkjv)*

### Ezekiel 17:15

*But he rebelled against him by sending his ambassadors to Egypt, that they might give him horses and many people. Will he prosper? Will he who does such things escape? Can he break a covenant and still be delivered? (nkjv)*

### Daniel 8:24

*His power shall be mighty, but not by his own power; he shall destroy fearfully, and shall prosper and thrive; he shall destroy the mighty, and also the holy people. (nkjv)*

**Daniel 8:25**

*Through his cunning he shall cause deceit to prosper under his rule; and he shall exalt himself in his heart. He shall destroy many in their prosperity. He shall even rise against the Prince of princes; but he shall be broken without human means. (nkjv)*

**Daniel 11:27**

*Both these kings' hearts shall be bent on evil, and they shall speak lies at the same table; but it shall not prosper, for the end will still be at the appointed time. (nkjv)*

**Daniel 11:36**

*Then the king shall do according to his own will: he shall exalt and magnify himself above every god, shall speak blasphemies against the God of gods, and shall prosper till the wrath has been accomplished; for what has been determined shall be done. (nkjv)*

**1 Corinthians 16:2**

*On the first day of the week let each one of you lay something aside, storing up as he may prosper, that there be no collections when I come. (nkjv)*

### 3 John 1:2

*Beloved, I pray that you may prosper in all things and be in health, just as your soul prospers. (nkjv)*

# Scriptures on God's Provision and Abundance

**Genesis 27:28**

*May God give you of heaven's dew and of earth's richness—an abundance of grain and new wine.*

**Genesis 41:29**

*Seven years of great abundance are coming throughout the land of Egypt.*

**Genesis 41:30–32**

*But seven years of famine will follow them. Then all the abundance in Egypt will be forgotten, and the famine will ravage the land. The abundance in the land will not be remembered, because the famine that follows it will be so severe.*

**Genesis 41:47**

*During the seven years of abundance the land produced plentifully.*

### Genesis 41:48

*Joseph collected all the food produced in those seven years of abundance in Egypt and stored it in the cities. In each city he put the food grown in the fields surrounding it.*

### Genesis 41:53

*They will summon peoples to the mountain and there offer sacrifices of righteousness; they will feast on the abundance of the seas, on the treasures hidden in the sand.*

### Numbers 24:7

*Water will flow from their buckets; their seed will have abundant water. "Their king will be greater than Agag; their kingdom will be exalted."*

### Deuteronomy 6:3

*Listen obediently, Israel. Do what you're told so that you'll have a good life, a life of abundance and bounty, just as God promised, in a land abounding in milk and honey. (The Message)*

### Deuteronomy 28:11

*The Lord will grant you abundant prosperity—in the fruit of your womb, the young of your livestock and the*

*crops of your ground—in the land he swore to your fore-*
*fathers to give you.*

**Deuteronomy 32:2**

*Let my teaching fall like rain and my words descend like*
*dew, like showers on new grass, like abundant rain on*
*tender plants.*

**1 Chronicles 29:16**

*O Lord our God, as for all this abundance that we have*
*provided for building you a temple for your Holy Name,*
*it comes from your hand, and all of it belongs to you.*

**1 Chronicles 29:21**

*The next day they made sacrifices to the Lord and pre-*
*sented burnt offerings to him: a thousand bulls, a thou-*
*sand rams and a thousand male lambs, together with*
*their drink offerings, and other sacrifices in abundance*
*for all Israel.*

**2 Chronicles 11:23**

*He acted wisely, dispersing some of his sons through-*
*out the districts of Judah and Benjamin, and to all the*
*fortified cities. He gave them abundant provisions and*
*took many wives for them.*

### 2 Chronicles 29:35

*There were burnt offerings in abundance, together with the fat of the fellowship offerings and the drink offerings that accompanied the burnt offerings. So the service of the temple of the Lord was reestablished.*

### Nehemiah 5:18

*Each day one ox, six choice sheep and some poultry were prepared for me, and every ten days an abundant supply of wine of all kinds. In spite of all this, I never demanded the food allotted to the governor, because the demands were heavy on these people.*

### Nehemiah 9:25

*They captured fortified cities and fertile land; they took possession of houses filled with all kinds of good things, wells already dug, vineyards, olive groves and fruit trees in abundance. They ate to the full and were well-nourished; they reveled in your great goodness.*

### Nehemiah 9:37

*Because of our sins, its abundant harvest goes to the kings you have placed over us. They rule over our bodies and our cattle as they please. We are in great distress.*

**Esther 1:7**

*Wine was served in goblets of gold, each one different from the other, and the royal wine was abundant, in keeping with the king's liberality.*

**Job 36:28**

*The clouds pour down their moisture and abundant showers fall on mankind.*

**Job 36:31**

*This is the way he governs the nations and provides food in abundance.*

**Psalm 36:8**

*They feast on the abundance of your house; you give them drink from your river of delights.*

**Psalm 65:11**

*You crown the year with your bounty, and your carts overflow with abundance.*

**Psalm 66:12**

*You let men ride over our heads; we went through fire and water, but you brought us to a place of abundance.*

**Psalm 68:9**

*You gave abundant showers, O God; you refreshed your weary inheritance.*

**Psalm 73:10**

*Therefore their people turn to them and drink up waters in abundance.*

**Psalm 78:15**

*He split the rocks in the desert and gave them water as abundant as the seas.*

**Psalm 132:15**

*I will bless her with abundant provisions; her poor will I satisfy with food.*

**Psalm 144:13**

*Our barns will be filled with every kind of provision.*

## Psalm 145:7

*They will celebrate your abundant goodness and joyfully sing of your righteousness.*

## Proverbs 12:11

*He who works his land will have abundant food, but he who chases fantasies lacks judgment.*

## Proverbs 13:23

*A poor man's field may produce abundant food, but injustice sweeps it away.*

## Proverbs 14:4

*Where there are no oxen, the manger is empty, but from the strength of an ox comes an abundant harvest.*

## Proverbs 20:15

*Gold there is, and rubies in abundance, but lips that speak knowledge are a rare jewel.*

## Proverbs 28:19

*He who works his land will have abundant food, but the one who chases fantasies will have his fill of poverty.*

### Ecclesiastes 5:12

*The sleep of a laborer is sweet, whether he eats little or much, but the abundance of a rich man permits him no sleep.*

### Isaiah 7:22

*And because of the abundance of the milk they give, he will have curds to eat. All who remain in the land will eat curds and honey.*

### Isaiah 23:18

*Yet her profit and her earnings will be set apart for the Lord; they will not be stored up or hoarded. Her profits will go to those who live before the Lord, for abundant food and fine clothes.*

### Isaiah 30:23

*God will provide rain for the seeds you sow. The grain that grows will be abundant. Your cattle will range far and wide. (The Message)*

### Isaiah 30:33

*Topheth has long been prepared; it has been made ready for the king. Its fire pit has been made deep and wide, with an abundance of fire and wood; the breath of the Lord, like a stream of burning sulfur, sets it ablaze.*

## Isaiah 33:23

*Your rigging hangs loose: The mast is not held secure, the sail is not spread. Then an abundance of spoils will be divided and even the lame will carry off plunder.*

## Isaiah 66:11

*"For you will nurse and be satisfied at her comforting breasts; you will drink deeply and delight in her overflowing abundance."*

## Jeremiah 2:22

*"Although you wash yourself with soda and use an abundance of soap, the stain of your guilt is still before me," declares the Sovereign Lord.*

## Jeremiah 31:14

*"I will satisfy the priests with abundance, and my people will be filled with my bounty," declares the Lord.*

## Jeremiah 33:6

*"Nevertheless, I will bring health and healing to it; I will heal my people and will let them enjoy abundant peace and security."*

### Jeremiah 33:9

*"Then this city will bring me renown, joy, praise and honor before all nations on earth that hear of all the good things I do for it; and they will be in awe and will tremble at the abundant prosperity and peace I provide for it."*

### Jeremiah 40:12

*They all came back to the land of Judah, to Gedaliah at Mizpah, from all the countries where they had been scattered. And they harvested an abundance of wine and summer fruit.*

### Ezekiel 17:5

*He took some of the seed of your land and put it in fertile soil. He planted it like a willow by abundant water.*

### Ezekiel 17:8

*It had been planted in good soil by abundant water so that it would produce branches, bear fruit and become a splendid vine.*

### Ezekiel 19:10

*Your mother was like a vine in your vineyard planted by the water; it was fruitful and full of branches because of abundant water.*

**Ezekiel 31:5**

*So it towered higher than all the trees of the field; its boughs increased and its branches grew long, spreading because of abundant waters.*

**Ezekiel 31:7**

*It was majestic in beauty, with its spreading boughs, for its roots went down to abundant waters.*

**Ezekiel 31:9**

*I made it beautiful with abundant branches, the envy of all the trees of Eden in the garden of God.*

**Ezekiel 31:15**

*This is what the Sovereign Lord says: On the day it was brought down to the grave I covered the deep springs with mourning for it; I held back its streams, and its abundant waters were restrained. Because of it I clothed Lebanon with gloom, and all the trees of the field withered away.*

**Ezekiel 32:13**

*I will destroy all her cattle from beside abundant waters no longer to be stirred by the foot of man or muddied by the hoofs of cattle.*

### Ezekiel 32:15

*When I turn Egypt back to the wild and strip her clean of all her abundant produce, when I strike dead all who live there, then they'll realize that I am God. (The Message)*

### Daniel 4:12

*Its leaves were beautiful, its fruit abundant, and on it was food for all. Under it the beasts of the field found shelter, and the birds of the air lived in its branches; from it every creature was fed.*

### Daniel 4:21

*With beautiful leaves and abundant fruit, providing food for all, giving shelter to the beasts of the field, and having nesting places in its branches for the birds of the air.*

### Joel 2:23

*Be glad, O people of Zion, rejoice in the Lord your God, for he has given you the autumn rains in righteousness. He sends you abundant showers, both autumn and spring rains, as before.*

## Matthew 13:12

*"Whoever has will be given more, and he will have an abundance. Whoever does not have, even what he has will be taken from him."*

## Matthew 25:29

*"For everyone who has will be given more, and he will have an abundance. Whoever does not have, even what he has will be taken from him."*

## Luke 12:15

*Then he said to them, "Watch out! Be on your guard against all kinds of greed; a man's life does not consist in the abundance of his possessions."*

## Luke 21:4

*"For they all gave out of their abundance (their surplus); but she has contributed out of her lack and her want, putting in all that she had on which to live." (amp)*

## John 10:10

*"The thief comes only in order to steal and kill and destroy. I came that they may have and enjoy life, and have it in abundance (to the full, till it overflows)." (amp)*

### John 15:5

*"I am the Vine, you are the branches. When you're joined with me and I with you, the relation intimate and organic, the harvest is sure to be abundant. Separated, you can't produce a thing." (The Message)*

### Romans 5:17

*For if, by the trespass of the one man, death reigned through that one man, how much more will those who receive God's abundant provision of grace and of the gift of righteousness reign in life through the one man, Jesus Christ.*

### 2 Corinthians 9:8

*And God is able to make all grace (every favor and earthly blessing) come to you in abundance, so that you may always and under all circumstances and whatever the need be self-sufficient [possessing enough to require no aid or support and furnished in abundance for every good work and charitable donation]. (amp)*

### Philippians 4:12

*I know how to be abased and live humbly in straitened circumstances, and I know also how to enjoy plenty and live in abundance. I have learned in any and all circumstances the secret of facing every situation, whether well-*

*fed or going hungry, having a sufficiency and enough to spare or going without and being in want. (amp)*

**1 Peter 1:2**

*Who have been chosen according to the foreknowledge of God the Father, through the sanctifying work of the Spirit, for obedience to Jesus Christ and sprinkling by his blood: Grace and peace be yours in abundance.*

**2 Peter 1:2**

*Grace and peace be yours in abundance through the knowledge of God and of Jesus our Lord.*

**Jude 1:2**

*Mercy, peace and love be yours in abundance.*

# Scriptures on Financial Topics

## Accounting

### Daniel 6:1–3

*It pleased Darius to appoint 120 satraps to rule throughout the kingdom, with three administrators over them, one of whom was Daniel. The satraps were made accountable to them so that the king might not suffer loss.*

### Matthew 18:23

*"Therefore, the kingdom of heaven is like a king who wanted to settle accounts with his servants."*

### Matthew 25:14–30

*"Again, it will be like a man going on a journey, who called his servants and entrusted his property to them. To one he gave five talents of money, to another two talents, and to another one talent, each according to his ability. Then he went on his journey. The man who had received the five talents went at once and put his money to work and gained five more. So also, the one with the two talents gained two more. But the man who had received the one talent went off, dug a hole in the ground and hid his master's money.*

"After a long time the master of those servants returned and settled accounts with them. The man who had received the five talents brought the other five. 'Master,' he said, 'you entrusted me with five talents. See, I have gained five more.'

"His master replied, 'Well done, good and faithful servant! You have been faithful with a few things; I will put you in charge of many things. Come and share your master's happiness!'

"The man with the two talents also came. 'Master,' he said, 'you entrusted me with two talents; see, I have gained two more.'

"His master replied, 'Well done, good and faithful servant! You have been faithful with a few things; I will put you in charge of many things. Come and share your master's happiness!'

"Then the man who had received the one talent came. 'Master,' he said, 'I knew that you are a hard man, harvesting where you have not sown and gathering where you have not scattered seed. So I was afraid and went out and hid your talent in the ground. See, here is what belongs to you.'

"His master replied, 'You wicked, lazy servant! So you knew that I harvest where I have not sown and gather where I have not scattered seed? Well then, you should *have put my money on deposit with the bankers, so that when I returned I would have received it back with interest.*

*"'Take the talent from him and give it to the one who has the ten talents. For everyone who has will be given more, and he will have an abundance. Whoever does not have, even what he has will be taken from him. And throw that worthless servant outside, into the darkness, where there will be weeping and gnashing of teeth.'"*

## Romans 14:12

*So then, each of us will give an account of himself to God.*

# Against the Unfortunate

## Deuteronomy 24:14

*Do not take advantage of a hired man who is poor and needy, whether he is a brother Israelite or an alien living in one of your towns.*

## Psalm 10:2

*In his arrogance the wicked man hunts down the weak, who are caught in the schemes he devises.*

### Psalm 12:5

*"Because of the oppression of the weak and the groaning of the needy, I will now arise," says the Lord. "I will protect them from those who malign them."*

### Proverbs 14:20–21, 31

*The poor are shunned even by their neighbors, but the rich have many friends. He who despises his neighbor sins, but blessed is he who is kind to the needy. He who oppresses the poor shows contempt for their Maker, but whoever is kind to the needy honors God.*

### Proverbs 21:13

*If a man shuts his ears to the cry of the poor, he too will cry out and not be answered.*

### Proverbs 22:16

*He who oppresses the poor to increase his wealth and he who gives gifts to the rich—both come to poverty.*

### Proverbs 24:23

*These also are sayings of the wise: To show partiality in judging is not good.*

**Proverbs 28:8**

*He who increases his wealth by exorbitant interest amasses it for another, who will be kind to the poor.*

**Matthew 18:23, 34**

*Therefore, the kingdom of heaven is like a king who wanted to settle accounts with his servants. In anger his master turned him over to the jailers to be tortured, until he should pay back all he owed.*

**Luke 11:42**

*"Woe to you Pharisees, because you give God a tenth of your mint, rue and all other kinds of garden herbs, but you neglect justice and the love of God. You should have practiced the latter without leaving the former undone."*

**Luke 16:19–25**

*"There was a rich man who was dressed in purple and fine linen and lived in luxury every day. At his gate was laid a beggar named Lazarus, covered with sores and longing to eat what fell from the rich man's table. Even the dogs came and licked his sores.*

*"The time came when the beggar died and the angels carried him to Abraham's side. The rich man also died*

*and was buried. In hell, where he was in torment, he looked up and saw Abraham far away, with Lazarus by his side. So he called to him, 'Father Abraham, have pity on me and send Lazarus to dip the tip of his finger in water and cool my tongue, because I am in agony in this fire.'*

*"But Abraham replied, 'Son, remember that in your lifetime you received your good things, while Lazarus received bad things, but now he is comforted here and you are in agony.'"*

## Attitudes, Viewpoints, and Actions

### Psalm 112:2–3

*His children will be mighty in the land; the generation of the upright will be blessed. Wealth and riches are in his house, and his righteousness endures forever.*

### Psalm 112:9

*He has scattered abroad his gifts to the poor, his righteousness endures forever; his horn will be lifted high in honor.*

### Proverbs 10:4

*Lazy hands make a man poor, but diligent hands bring wealth.*

## Proverbs 13:4, 11

*The sluggard craves and gets nothing, but the desires of the diligent are fully satisfied. Dishonest money dwindles away, but he who gathers money little by little makes it grow.*

## Proverbs 24:10

*If you falter in times of trouble, how small is your strength!*

## Proverbs 28:27

*He who gives to the poor will lack nothing, but he who closes his eyes to them receives many curses.*

## Ecclesiastes 5:12

*The sleep of a laborer is sweet, whether he eats little or much, but the abundance of a rich man permits him no sleep.*

## Malachi 3:5

*"So I will come near to you for judgment. I will be quick to testify against sorcerers, adulterers and perjurers, against those who defraud laborers of their wages, who oppress the widows and the fatherless, and deprive aliens of justice, but do not fear me," says the Lord Almighty.*

**Luke 6:35a**

*But love your enemies, do good to them, and lend to them without expecting to get anything back.*

**Romans 12:11**

*Never be lacking in zeal, but keep your spiritual fervor, serving the Lord.*

**Ephesians 4:28**

*He who has been stealing must steal no longer, but must work, doing something useful with his own hands, that he may have something to share with those in need.*

## Blamelessness

**Psalm 1:1–2**

*Blessed is the man who does not walk in the counsel of the wicked or stand in the way of sinners or sit in the seat of mockers. But his delight is in the law of the Lord, and on his law he meditates day and night.*

**Psalm 37:37**

*Consider the blameless, observe the upright; there is a future for the man of peace.*

**Psalm 112:6**

*Surely he will never be shaken; a righteous man will be remembered forever.*

**Proverbs 10:16**

*The wages of the righteous bring them life, but the income of the wicked brings them punishment.*

**Proverbs 11:4**

*Wealth is worthless in the day of wrath, but righteousness delivers from death.*

**Proverbs 12:12**

*The wicked desire the plunder of evil men, but the root of the righteous flourishes.*

**Proverbs 16:8, 11**

*Better a little with righteousness than much gain with injustice. Honest scales and balances are from the Lord; all the weights in the bag are of his making.*

**Proverbs 19:1**

*Better a poor man whose walk is blameless than a fool whose lips are perverse.*

### Proverbs 21:3

*To do what is right and just is more acceptable to the Lord than sacrifice.*

### Proverbs 22:1

*A good name is more desirable than great riches; to be esteemed is better than silver or gold.*

### Proverbs 28:6, 13

*Better a poor man whose walk is blameless than a rich man whose ways are perverse. He who conceals his sins does not prosper, but whoever confesses and renounces them finds mercy.*

### Matthew 7:20

*Thus, by their fruit you will recognize them.*

### Luke 3:12–14

*Tax collectors also came to be baptized. "Teacher," they asked, "what should we do?" "Don't collect any more than you are required to," he told them. Then some soldiers asked him, "And what should we do?" He replied, "Don't extort money and don't accuse people falsely—be content with your pay."*

## Luke 8:15

*"But the seed on good soil stands for those with a noble and good heart, who hear the word, retain it, and by persevering produce a crop."*

## Luke 12:57–58

*"Why don't you judge for yourselves what is right? As you are going with your adversary to the magistrate, try hard to be reconciled to him on the way, or he may drag you off to the judge, and the judge turn you over to the officer, and the officer throw you into prison."*

## Luke 20:22–25

*"Is it right for us to pay taxes to Caesar or not?" He saw through their duplicity and said to them, "Show me a denarius. Whose portrait and inscription are on it?" "Caesar's," they replied. He said to them, "Then give to Caesar what is Caesar's, and to God what is God's."*

## Romans 13:7

*Give everyone what you owe him: If you owe taxes, pay taxes; if revenue, then revenue; if respect, then respect; if honor, then honor.*

### Galatians 6:9

*Let us not become weary in doing good, for at the proper time we will reap a harvest if we do not give up.*

# Borrowing

### Exodus 22:14

*If a man borrows an animal from his neighbor and it is injured or dies while the owner is not present, he must make restitution.*

### Deuteronomy 15:1–11

*At the end of every seven years you must cancel debts. This is how it is to be done: Every creditor shall cancel the loan he has made to his fellow Israelite. He shall not require payment from his fellow Israelite or brother, because the Lord's time for canceling debts has been proclaimed. You may require payment from a foreigner, but you must cancel any debt your brother owes you. However, there should be no poor among you, for in the land the Lord your God is giving you to possess as your inheritance, he will richly bless you, if only you fully obey the Lord your God and are careful to follow all these commands I am giving you today. For the Lord your God will bless you as he has promised, and you will lend to many nations but will borrow from none. You will rule over many nations but none will rule over you. If there is a poor man among your broth-*

*ers in any of the towns of the land that the Lord your God is giving you, do not be hardhearted or tightfisted toward your poor brother. Rather be openhanded and freely lend him whatever he needs. Be careful not to harbor this wicked thought: "The seventh year, the year for canceling debts, is near," so that you do not show ill will toward your needy brother and give him nothing. He may then appeal to the Lord against you, and you will be found guilty of sin. Give generously to him and do so without a grudging heart; then because of this the Lord your God will bless you in all your work and in everything you put your hand to. There will always be poor people in the land. Therefore I command you to be openhanded toward your brothers and toward the poor and needy in your land.*

## Psalm 37:25

*I was young and now I am old, yet I have never seen the righteous forsaken or their children begging bread.*

## Proverbs 3:27–28

*Do not withhold good from those who deserve it, when it is in your power to act. Do not say to your neighbor, "Come back later; I'll give it tomorrow"—when you now have it with you.*

## Proverbs 22:7

*The rich rule over the poor, and the borrower is servant to the lender.*

### Matthew 5:25–26, 40

*"Settle matters quickly with your adversary who is taking you to court. Do it while you are still with him on the way, or he may hand you over to the judge, and the judge may hand you over to the officer, and you may be thrown into prison. I tell you the truth, you will not get out until you have paid the last penny. And if someone wants to sue you and take your tunic, let him have your cloak as well."*

### Matthew 18:23–35

*"Therefore, the kingdom of heaven is like a king who wanted to settle accounts with his servants. As he began the settlement, a man who owed him ten thousand talents was brought to him. Since he was not able to pay, the master ordered that he and his wife and his children and all that he had be sold to repay the debt.*

*"The servant fell on his knees before him. 'Be patient with me,' he begged, 'and I will pay back everything.' The servant's master took pity on him, canceled the debt and let him go.*

*"But when that servant went out, he found one of his fellow servants who owed him a hundred denarii. He grabbed him and began to choke him. 'Pay back what you owe me!' he demanded.*

*"His fellow servant fell to his knees and begged him, 'Be patient with me, and I will pay you back.'*

*"But he refused. Instead, he went off and had the man thrown into prison until he could pay the debt. When the other servants saw what had happened, they were greatly distressed and went and told their master everything that had happened.*

*"Then the master called the servant in. 'You wicked servant,' he said, 'I canceled all that debt of yours because you begged me to. Shouldn't you have had mercy on your fellow servant just as I had on you?' In anger his master turned him over to the jailers to be tortured, until he should pay back all he owed.*

*"This is how my heavenly Father will treat each of you unless you forgive your brother from your heart."*

## Budgeting

### Proverbs 16:9

*In his heart a man plans his course, but the Lord determines his steps.*

### Proverbs 19:21

*Many are the plans in a man's heart, but it is the Lord's purpose that prevails.*

### Proverbs 22:3

*A prudent man sees danger and takes refuge, but the simple keep going and suffer for it.*

### Proverbs 24:3–4

*By wisdom a house is built, and through understanding it is established; through knowledge its rooms are filled with rare and beautiful treasures.*

### Proverbs 27:12

*The prudent see danger and take refuge, but the simple keep going and suffer for it.*

### Luke 12:16–21

*And he told them this parable: "The ground of a certain rich man produced a good crop. He thought to himself, What shall I do? I have no place to store my crops.*

*"Then he said, 'This is what I'll do. I will tear down my barns and build bigger ones, and there I will store all my grain and my goods. And I'll say to myself, You have*

*plenty of good things laid up for many years. Take life easy; eat, drink and be merry.*

*"But God said to him, 'You fool! This very night your life will be demanded from you. Then who will get what you have prepared for yourself?'*

*"This is how it will be with anyone who stores up things for himself but is not rich toward God."*

## Luke 14:28–30

*"Suppose one of you wants to build a tower. Will he not first sit down and estimate the cost to see if he has enough money to complete it? For if he lays the foundation and is not able to finish it, everyone who sees it will ridicule him, saying, 'This fellow began to build and was not able to finish.'"*

## Luke 16:1–8

*Jesus told his disciples: "There was a rich man whose manager was accused of wasting his possessions. So he called him in and asked him, 'What is this I hear about you? Give an account of your management, because you cannot be manager any longer.'*

*"The manager said to himself, 'What shall I do now? My master is taking away my job. I'm not strong enough to dig, and I'm ashamed to beg—I know what I'll do so*

*that, when I lose my job here, people will welcome me into their houses.'*

"*So he called in each one of his master's debtors. He asked the first, 'How much do you owe my master?'*

"'*Eight hundred gallons of olive oil,' he replied.*

"*The manager told him, 'Take your bill, sit down quickly, and make it four hundred.'*

"*Then he asked the second, 'And how much do you owe?'*

"'*A thousand bushels of wheat,' he replied.*

"*He told him, 'Take your bill and make it eight hundred.'*

"*The master commended the dishonest manager because he had acted shrewdly. For the people of this world are more shrewd in dealing with their own kind than are the people of the light.*"

**1 Corinthians 16:1–2**

*Now about the collection for God's people: Do what I told the Galatian churches to do. On the first day of every week, each one of you should set aside a sum of money in keeping with his income, saving it up, so that when I come no collections will have to be made.*

# Caution

**Proverbs 8:12**

*I, wisdom, dwell together with prudence; I possess knowledge and discretion.*

**Proverbs 12:16, 23**

*A fool shows his annoyance at once, but a prudent man overlooks an insult. A prudent man keeps his knowledge to himself, but the heart of fools blurts out folly.*

**Proverbs 13:16**

*Every prudent man acts out of knowledge, but a fool exposes his folly.*

### Proverbs 14:8, 15, 18

*The wisdom of the prudent is to give thought to their ways, but the folly of fools is deception. A simple man believes anything, but a prudent man gives thought to his steps. The simple inherit folly, but the prudent are crowned with knowledge.*

### Proverbs 15:5

*A fool spurns his father's discipline, but whoever heeds correction shows prudence.*

### Proverbs 16:21

*The wise in heart are called discerning, and pleasant words promote instruction.*

### Proverbs 18:15

*The heart of the discerning acquires knowledge; the ears of the wise seek it out.*

### Proverbs 22:3

*A prudent man sees danger and takes refuge, but the simple keep going and suffer for it.*

**Proverbs 27:12**

*The prudent see danger and take refuge, but the simple keep going and suffer for it.*

**Hosea 14:9**

*Who is wise? He will realize these things. Who is discerning? He will understand them. The ways of the Lord are right; the righteous walk in them, but the rebellious stumble in them.*

**Amos 5:13**

*This is what the Sovereign Lord says: "The city that marches out a thousand strong for Israel will have only a hundred left; the town that marches out a hundred strong will have only ten left."*

## Contentment

**Joshua 7:7**

*And Joshua said, "Ah, Sovereign Lord, why did you ever bring this people across the Jordan to deliver us into the hands of the Amorites to destroy us? If only we had been content to stay on the other side of the Jordan!"*

### Proverbs 30:7–9

*"Two things I ask of you, O Lord; do not refuse me before I die: Keep falsehood and lies far from me; give me neither poverty nor riches, but give me only my daily bread. Otherwise, I may have too much and disown you and say, 'Who is the Lord?' Or I may become poor and steal, and so dishonor the name of my God."*

### Matthew 20:1–16

*"For the kingdom of heaven is like a landowner who went out early in the morning to hire men to work in his vineyard. He agreed to pay them a denarius for the day and sent them into his vineyard.*

*"About the third hour he went out and saw others standing in the marketplace doing nothing. He told them, 'You also go and work in my vineyard, and I will pay you whatever is right.' So they went.*

*"He went out again about the sixth hour and the ninth hour and did the same thing. About the eleventh hour he went out and found still others standing around. He asked them, 'Why have you been standing here all day long doing nothing?'*

*"'Because no one has hired us,' they answered. "He said to them, 'You also go and work in my vineyard.'*

*"When evening came, the owner of the vineyard said to his foreman, 'Call the workers and pay them their wages, beginning with the last ones hired and going on to the first.'*

*"The workers who were hired about the eleventh hour came and each received a denarius. So when those came who were hired first, they expected to receive more. But each one of them also received a denarius. When they received it, they began to grumble against the landowner. 'These men who were hired last worked only one hour,' they said, 'and you have made them equal to us who have borne the burden of the work and the heat of the day.'*

*"But he answered one of them, 'Friend, I am not being unfair to you. Didn't you agree to work for a denarius? Take your pay and go. I want to give the man who was hired last the same as I gave you. Don't I have the right to do what I want with my own money? Or are you envious because I am generous?'*

*"So the last will be first, and the first will be last."*

## 2 Corinthians 6:10

*Sorrowful, yet always rejoicing; poor, yet making many rich; having nothing, and yet possessing everything.*

### Philippians 4:11–12

*I am not saying this because I am in need, for I have learned to be content whatever the circumstances. I know what it is to be in need, and I know what it is to have plenty. I have learned the secret of being content in any and every situation, whether well fed or hungry, whether living in plenty or in want.*

### Colossians 3:2

*Set your minds on things above, not on earthly things.*

### 1 Thessalonians 5:16–18

*Be joyful always; pray continually; give thanks in all circumstances, for this is God's will for you in Christ Jesus.*

### 1 Timothy 6:6–10

*But godliness with contentment is great gain. For we brought nothing into the world, and we can take nothing out of it. But if we have food and clothing, we will be content with that. People who want to get rich fall into temptation and a trap and into many foolish and harmful desires that plunge men into ruin and destruction. For the love of money is a root of all kinds of evil. Some people, eager for money, have wandered from the faith and pierced themselves with many griefs.*

**Hebrews 13:5**

*Keep your lives free from the love of money and be content with what you have, because God has said, "Never will I leave you; never will I forsake you."*

# Counsel

**Proverbs 3:13**

*Blessed is the man who finds wisdom, the man who gains understanding,*

**Proverbs 12:5, 15**

*The plans of the righteous are just, but the advice of the wicked is deceitful. The way of a fool seems right to him, but a wise man listens to advice.*

**Proverbs 13:20**

*He who walks with the wise grows wise, but a companion of fools suffers harm.*

**Proverbs 14:7**

*Stay away from a foolish man, for you will not find knowledge on his lips.*

### Proverbs 15:22

*Plans fail for lack of counsel, but with many advisers they succeed.*

### Proverbs 19:20

*Listen to advice and accept instruction, and in the end you will be wise.*

### Proverbs 24:3, 6

*By wisdom a house is built, and through understanding it is established; for waging war you need guidance, and for victory many advisers.*

### Proverbs 27:9

*Perfume and incense bring joy to the heart, and the pleasantness of one's friend springs from his earnest counsel.*

## Cosigning Notes

### Proverbs 6:1–5

*My son, if you have put up security for your neighbor, if you have struck hands in pledge for another, if you have been trapped by what you said, ensnared by the words of your mouth, then do this, my son, to free yourself, since you have fallen into your neighbor's hands: Go and humble yourself; press your plea with your neighbor! Allow no sleep to your eyes, no slumber to your eyelids. Free yourself, like a gazelle from the hand of the hunter, like a bird from the snare of the fowler.*

## Proverbs 11:15

*He who puts up security for another will surely suffer, but whoever refuses to strike hands in pledge is safe.*

## Proverbs 17:18

*A man lacking in judgment strikes hands in pledge and puts up security for his neighbor.*

## Proverbs 20:16

*Take the garment of one who puts up security for a stranger; hold it in pledge if he does it for a wayward woman.*

## Proverbs 22:26

*Do not be a man who strikes hands in pledge or puts up security for debts.*

**Proverbs 27:13**

*Take the garment of one who puts up security for a stranger; hold it in pledge if he does it for a wayward woman.*

# Debt

**Deuteronomy 15:6**

*For the Lord your God will bless you as he has promised, and you will lend to many nations but will borrow from none. You will rule over many nations but none will rule over you.*

**Deuteronomy 28:12–13**

*The Lord will open the heavens, the storehouse of his bounty, to send rain on your land in season and to bless all the work of your hands. You will lend to many nations but will borrow from none. The Lord will make you the head, not the tail. If you pay attention to the commands of the Lord your God that I give you this day and carefully follow them, you will always be at the top, never at the bottom.*

**2 Kings 4:1–7**

*The wife of a man from the company of the prophets cried out to Elisha, "Your servant my husband is dead, and you know that he revered the Lord. But now his creditor is coming to take my two boys as his slaves." Elisha replied to her, "How can I help you? Tell me, what do you have in your house?" "Your servant has nothing there at all," she said, "except a little oil." Elisha said, "Go around and ask all your neighbors for empty jars. Don't ask for just a few. Then go inside and shut the door behind you and your sons. Pour oil into all the jars, and as each is filled, put it to one side." She left him and afterward shut the door behind her and her sons. They brought the jars to her and she kept pouring. When all the jars were full, she said to her son, "Bring me another one." But he replied, "There is not a jar left." Then the oil stopped flowing. She went and told the man of God, and he said, "Go, sell the oil and pay your debts. You and your sons can live on what is left."*

## Psalm 37:21

*The wicked borrow and do not repay, but the righteous give generously;*

## Proverbs 3:27–28

*Do not withhold good from those who deserve it, when it is in your power to act. Do not say to your neighbor, "Come back later; I'll give it tomorrow"—when you now have it with you.*

### Proverbs 6:1–3

*My son, if you have put up security for your neighbor, if you have struck hands in pledge for another, if you have been trapped by what you said, ensnared by the words of your mouth, then do this, my son, to free yourself, since you have fallen into your neighbor's hands: Go and humble yourself; press your plea with your neighbor!*

### Proverbs 11:15

*He who puts up security for another will surely suffer, but whoever refuses to strike hands in pledge is safe.*

### Proverbs 17:18

*A man lacking in judgment strikes hands in pledge and puts up security for his neighbor.*

### Proverbs 22:7

*The rich rule over the poor, and the borrower is servant to the lender.*

### Proverbs 27:13

*Take the garment of one who puts up security for a stranger; hold it in pledge if he does it for a wayward woman.*

**Matthew 5:25–26**

*"Settle matters quickly with your adversary who is taking you to court. Do it while you are still with him on the way, or he may hand you over to the judge, and the judge may hand you over to the officer, and you may be thrown into prison. I tell you the truth, you will not get out until you have paid the last penny."*

**Matthew 18:23**

*"Therefore, the kingdom of heaven is like a king who wanted to settle accounts with his servants."*

**Romans 13:8**

*Let no debt remain outstanding, except the continuing debt to love one another, for he who loves his fellowman has fulfilled the law.*

# Diligence

**Proverbs 6:4**

*Allow no sleep to your eyes, no slumber to your eyelids.*

### Proverbs 12:11, 24

*He who works his land will have abundant food, but he who chases fantasies lacks judgment. Diligent hands will rule, but laziness ends in slave labor.*

### Proverbs 13:11

*Dishonest money dwindles away, but he who gathers money little by little makes it grow.*

### Proverbs 14:4

*Where there are no oxen, the manger is empty, but from the strength of an ox comes an abundant harvest.*

### Proverbs 16:3

*Commit to the Lord whatever you do, and your plans will succeed.*

### Proverbs 21:5

*The plans of the diligent lead to profit as surely as haste leads to poverty.*

### Proverbs 24:3–4, 7

*By wisdom a house is built, and through understanding it is established; through knowledge its rooms are filled with rare and beautiful treasures. Wisdom is too high for a fool; in the assembly at the gate he has nothing to say.*

### Matthew 20:13

*"But he answered one of them, 'Friend, I am not being unfair to you. Didn't you agree to work for a denarius?'"*

### 2 Timothy 2:6

*The hardworking farmer should be the first to receive a share of the crops.*

### 1 Thessalonians 4:11

*Make it your ambition to lead a quiet life, to mind your own business and to work with your hands, just as we told you.*

## Dishonesty

### Psalm 37:37

*Consider the blameless, observe the upright; there is a future for the man of peace.*

### Psalm 15:5

*Who lends his money without usury and does not accept a bribe against the innocent. He who does these things will never be shaken.*

### Psalm 62:10–12

*Do not trust in extortion or take pride in stolen goods; though your riches increase, do not set your heart on them. One thing God has spoken, two things have I heard: that you, O God, are strong, and that you, O Lord, are loving. Surely you will reward each person according to what he has done.*

### Proverbs 10:15–16

*The wealth of the rich is their fortified city, but poverty is the ruin of the poor. The wages of the righteous bring them life, but the income of the wicked brings them punishment.*

### Proverbs 11:1, 16, 18

*The Lord abhors dishonest scales, but accurate weights are his delight. A kindhearted woman gains respect, but ruthless men gain only wealth. The wicked man earns deceptive wages, but he who sows righteousness reaps a sure reward.*

**Proverbs 12:3, 12**

*A man cannot be established through wickedness, but the righteous cannot be uprooted. The wicked desire the plunder of evil men, but the root of the righteous flourishes.*

**Proverbs 13:7, 11**

*One man pretends to be rich, yet has nothing; another pretends to be poor, yet has great wealth. Dishonest money dwindles away, but he who gathers money little by little makes it grow.*

**Proverbs 15:6, 27**

*The house of the righteous contains great treasure, but the income of the wicked brings them trouble. A greedy man brings trouble to his family, but he who hates bribes will live.*

**Proverbs 16:2, 11**

*All a man's ways seem innocent to him, but motives are weighed by the Lord. Honest scales and balances are from the Lord; all the weights in the bag are of his making.*

**Proverbs 17:2**

*A wise servant will rule over a disgraceful son, and will share the inheritance as one of the brothers.*

**Proverbs 20:21**

*An inheritance quickly gained at the beginning will not be blessed at the end.*

**Proverbs 22:28**

*Do not move an ancient boundary stone set up by your forefathers.*

**Proverbs 24:16, 19–20**

*For though a righteous man falls seven times, he rises again, but the wicked are brought down by calamity. Do not fret because of evil men or be envious of the wicked, for the evil man has no future hope, and the lamp of the wicked will be snuffed out.*

**Proverbs 28:6, 18**

*Better a poor man whose walk is blameless than a rich man whose ways are perverse. He whose walk is blameless is kept safe, but he whose ways are perverse will suddenly fall.*

**Jeremiah 9:4**

*Beware of your friends; do not trust your brothers. For every brother is a deceiver, and every friend a slanderer.*

**Matthew 18:7**

*Woe to the world because of the things that cause people to sin! Such things must come, but woe to the man through whom they come!*

**Matthew 27:5**

*So Judas threw the money into the temple and left. Then he went away and hanged himself.*

**Luke 9:25**

*What good is it for a man to gain the whole world, and yet lose or forfeit his very self?*

**Luke 11:42**

*Woe to you Pharisees, because you give God a tenth of your mint, rue and all other kinds of garden herbs, but you neglect justice and the love of God. You should have practiced the latter without leaving the former undone.*

### Luke 16:1, 10–14

*Jesus told his disciples: "There was a rich man whose manager was accused of wasting his possessions.*

*"Whoever can be trusted with very little can also be trusted with much, and whoever is dishonest with very little will also be dishonest with much. So if you have not been trustworthy in handling worldly wealth, who will trust you with true riches? And if you have not been trustworthy with someone else's property, who will give you property of your own?*

*"No servant can serve two masters. Either he will hate the one and love the other, or he will be devoted to the one and despise the other. You cannot serve both God and Money."*

*The Pharisees, who loved money, heard all this and were sneering at Jesus.*

### Luke 19:8

*But Zacchaeus stood up and said to the Lord, "Look, Lord! Here and now I give half of my possessions to the poor, and if I have cheated anybody out of anything, I will pay back four times the amount."*

**Luke 20:46–47**

*"Beware of the teachers of the law. They like to walk around in flowing robes and love to be greeted in the marketplaces and have the most important seats in the synagogues and the places of honor at banquets. They devour widows' houses and for a show make lengthy prayers. Such men will be punished most severely."*

**Romans 2:21–22**

*You, then, who teach others, do you not teach yourself? You who preach against stealing, do you steal? You who say that people should not commit adultery, do you commit adultery? You who abhor idols, do you rob temples?*

# Ego

**Psalm 75:4**

*To the arrogant I say, "Boast no more," and to the wicked, "Do not lift up your horns."*

**Psalm 107:40**

*He who pours contempt on nobles made them wander in a trackless waste.*

**Proverbs 11:2**

*When pride comes, then comes disgrace, but with humility comes wisdom.*

**Proverbs 12:9**

*Better to be a nobody and yet have a servant than pretend to be somebody and have no food.*

**Proverbs 15:25**

*The Lord tears down the proud man's house but he keeps the widow's boundaries intact.*

**Proverbs 16:18–19**

*Pride goes before destruction, a haughty spirit before a fall. Better to be lowly in spirit and among the oppressed than to share plunder with the proud.*

**Proverbs 18:12, 23**

*Before his downfall a man's heart is proud, but humility comes before honor. A poor man pleads for mercy, but a rich man answers harshly.*

**Proverbs 19:1**

*Better a poor man whose walk is blameless than a fool whose lips are perverse.*

**Proverbs 28:11**

*A rich man may be wise in his own eyes, but a poor man who has discernment sees through him.*

**Proverbs 29:23**

*A man's pride brings him low, but a man of lowly spirit gains honor.*

**Jeremiah 9:23**

*This is what the Lord says: "Let not the wise man boast of his wisdom or the strong man boast of his strength or the rich man boast of his riches."*

**Jeremiah 22:21**

*I warned you when you felt secure, but you said, "I will not listen!" This has been your way from your youth; you have not obeyed me.*

**Matthew 23:12**

*"For whoever exalts himself will be humbled, and whoever humbles himself will be exalted."*

**Luke 14:11**

*"For everyone who exalts himself will be humbled, and he who humbles himself will be exalted."*

**Philippians 2:3**

*Do nothing out of selfish ambition or vain conceit, but in humility consider others better than yourselves.*

**1 Timothy 6:17**

*Command those who are rich in this present world not to be arrogant nor to put their hope in wealth, which is so uncertain, but to put their hope in God, who richly provides us with everything for our enjoyment.*

# Envy

**Psalm 73:2**

*But as for me, my feet had almost slipped; I had nearly lost my foothold.*

**Proverbs 23:17**

*Do not let your heart envy sinners, but always be zealous for the fear of the Lord.*

**Proverbs 24:19**

*Do not fret because of evil men or be envious of the wicked,*

# Excellence

**Proverbs 18:9**

*One who is slack in his work is brother to one who destroys.*

**Proverbs 22:29**

*Do you see a man skilled in his work? He will serve before kings; he will not serve before obscure men.*

**Colossians 3:17, 23**

*And whatever you do, whether in word or deed, do it all in the name of the Lord Jesus, giving thanks to God the Father through him. Whatever you do, work at it with all your heart, as working for the Lord, not for men,*

**1 Peter 4:11**

*If anyone speaks, he should do it as one speaking the very words of God. If anyone serves, he should do it with the strength God provides, so that in all things God may be praised through Jesus Christ. To him be the glory and the power for ever and ever. Amen.*

# Getting the Facts

**Proverbs 14:8, 15**

*The wisdom of the prudent is to give thought to their ways, but the folly of fools is deception. A simple man believes anything, but a prudent man gives thought to his steps.*

**Proverbs 18:13**

*He who answers before listening—that is his folly and his shame.*

**Proverbs 19:2**

*It is not good to have zeal without knowledge, nor to be hasty and miss the way.*

**Proverbs 23:23**

*Buy the truth and do not sell it; get wisdom, discipline and understanding.*

**Proverbs 27:23–24**

*Be sure you know the condition of your flocks, give careful attention to your herds; for riches do not endure forever, and a crown is not secure for all generations.*

**James 1:5**

*If any of you lacks wisdom, he should ask God, who gives generously to all without finding fault, and it will be given to him.*

# Giving

**Isaiah 66:20**

*And they will bring all your brothers, from all the nations, to my holy mountain in Jerusalem as an offering to the Lord—on horses, in chariots and wagons, and on mules and camels," says the Lord. "They will bring them, as the Israelites bring their grain offerings, to the temple of the Lord in ceremonially clean vessels.*

**Psalm 96:7–8**

*Ascribe to the Lord, O families of nations, ascribe to the Lord glory and strength. Ascribe to the Lord the glory due his name; bring an offering and come into his courts.*

### Psalm 112:5

*Good will come to him who is generous and lends freely, who conducts his affairs with justice.*

### Proverbs 3:9–10

*Honor the Lord with your wealth, with the firstfruits of all your crops; then your barns will be filled to overflowing, and your vats will brim over with new wine.*

### Proverbs 11:24–26

*One man gives freely, yet gains even more; another withholds unduly, but comes to poverty. A generous man will prosper; he who refreshes others will himself be refreshed. People curse the man who hoards grain, but blessing crowns him who is willing to sell.*

### Proverbs 28:22

*A stingy man is eager to get rich and is unaware that poverty awaits him.*

### Mark 4:24

*"Consider carefully what you hear," he continued. "With the measure you use, it will be measured to you—and even more."*

### Mark 12:41–44

*Jesus sat down opposite the place where the offerings were put and watched the crowd putting their money into the temple treasury. Many rich people threw in large amounts. But a poor widow came and put in two very small copper coins, worth only a fraction of a penny. Calling his disciples to him, Jesus said, "I tell you the truth, this poor widow has put more into the treasury than all the others. They all gave out of their wealth; but she, out of her poverty, put in everything-all she had to live on."*

### Luke 6:38

*"Give, and it will be given to you. A good measure, pressed down, shaken together and running over, will be poured into your lap. For with the measure you use, it will be measured to you."*

### Acts 2:45

*Selling their possessions and goods, they gave to anyone as he had need.*

# Greed

### Psalm 73:2–3, 17, 20

*But as for me, my feet had almost slipped; I had nearly lost my foothold. For I envied the arrogant when I saw the prosperity of the wicked. Till I entered the sanctuary of God; then I understood their final destiny. As a dream when one awakes, so when you arise, O Lord, you will despise them as fantasies.*

### Proverbs 23:4–5

*Do not wear yourself out to get rich; have the wisdom to show restraint. Cast but a glance at riches, and they are gone, for they will surely sprout wings and fly off to the sky like an eagle.*

### Proverbs 28:25

*A greedy man stirs up dissension, but he who trusts in the Lord will prosper.*

### Luke 12:15

*Then he said to them, "Watch out! Be on your guard against all kinds of greed; a man's life does not consist in the abundance of his possessions."*

### Luke 18:24

*Jesus looked at him and said, "How hard it is for the rich to enter the kingdom of God!"*

### Ephesians 5:5

*For of this you can be sure: No immoral, impure or greedy person—such a man is an idolater—has any inheritance in the kingdom of Christ and of God.*

# Helping the Unfortunate

**Psalm 69:33**

*The Lord hears the needy and does not despise his captive people.*

**Psalm 72:1, 4–15, 17**

*Endow the king with your justice, O God, the royal son with your righteousness. He will defend the afflicted among the people and save the children of the needy; he will crush the oppressor. He will endure as long as the sun, as long as the moon, through all generations. He will be like rain falling on a mown field, like showers watering the earth. In his days the righteous will flourish; prosperity will abound till the moon is no more. He will rule from sea to sea and from the River to the ends of the earth. The desert tribes will bow before him and his enemies will lick the dust. The kings of Tarshish and of distant shores will bring tribute to him; the kings of Sheba and Seba will present him gifts. All kings will bow down to him and all nations will serve him. For he will deliver the needy who cry out, the afflicted who have no one to help. He will take pity on the weak and the needy and save the needy from death. He will rescue them from oppression and violence, for precious is their blood in his sight. Long may he live! May gold from Sheba be given him. May people ever pray for him and bless him all day long. May his name endure forever; may it continue as long as the sun. All nations will be blessed through him, and they will call him blessed.*

**Psalm 109:31**

*For he stands at the right hand of the needy one, to save his life from those who condemn him.*

**Proverbs 14:21**

*He who despises his neighbor sins, but blessed is he who is kind to the needy.*

**Proverbs 14:31**

*He who oppresses the poor shows contempt for their Maker, but whoever is kind to the needy honors God.*

**Matthew 5:42**

*"Give to the one who asks you, and do not turn away from the one who wants to borrow from you."*

**Matthew 6:19–20**

*"Do not store up for yourselves treasures on earth, where moth and rust destroy, and where thieves break in and steal. But store up for yourselves treasures in heaven, where moth and rust do not destroy, and where thieves do not break in and steal."*

## Matthew 10:42

*"And if anyone gives even a cup of cold water to one of these little ones because he is my disciple, I tell you the truth, he will certainly not lose his reward."*

## Luke 3:11

*John answered, "The man with two tunics should share with him who has none, and the one who has food should do the same."*

## Luke 9:48

*Then he said to them, "Whoever welcomes this little child in my name welcomes me; and whoever welcomes me welcomes the one who sent me. For he who is least among you all—he is the greatest."*

## Luke 10:35

*"The next day he took out two silver coins and gave them to the innkeeper. 'Look after him,' he said, 'and when I return, I will reimburse you for any extra expense you may have.'"*

## Luke 12:33

*"Sell your possessions and give to the poor. Provide purses for yourselves that will not wear out, a treasure*

*in heaven that will not be exhausted, where no thief comes near and no moth destroys."*

## Luke 19:8–9

*But Zacchaeus stood up and said to the Lord, "Look, Lord! Here and now I give half of my possessions to the poor, and if I have cheated anybody out of anything, I will pay back four times the amount." Jesus said to him, "Today salvation has come to this house, because this man, too, is a son of Abraham."*

## 1 Timothy 5:3, 8, 15–16

*Give proper recognition to those widows who are really in need. If anyone does not provide for his relatives, and especially for his immediate family, he has denied the faith and is worse than an unbeliever. Some have in fact already turned away to follow Satan. If any woman who is a believer has widows in her family, she should help them and not let the church be burdened with them, so that the church can help those widows who are really in need.*

## 1 John 3:17

*If anyone has material possessions and sees his brother in need but has no pity on him, how can the love of God be in him?*

# Hoarding

### Psalm 49:11, 16–17

*Their tombs will remain their houses for-*
*ever, their dwellings for endless gener*
*ations, though they had named lands after themselves.*
*Do not be overawed when a man grows rich, when the*
*splendor of his house increases; for he will take nothing*
*with him when he dies, his splendor will not descend*
*with him.*

### Proverbs 13:22

*A good man leaves an inheritance for his children's chil-*
*dren, but a sinner's wealth is stored up for the righ-*
*teous.*

### Proverbs 28:22

*A stingy man is eager to get rich and is unaware that*
*poverty awaits him.*

### Malachi 1:7, 9

*You place defiled food on my altar. "But you ask, 'How*
*have we defiled you?'*

*"By saying that the Lord's table is contemptible.*

*"Now implore God to be gracious to us. With such offerings from your hands, will he accept you?" says the Lord Almighty.*

## Malachi 3:8

*"Will a man rob God? Yet you rob me. But you ask, 'How do we rob you?' In tithes and offerings."*

## Matthew 6:24

*"No one can serve two masters. Either he will hate the one and love the other, or he will be devoted to the one and despise the other. You cannot serve both God and Money."*

## Matthew 19:23

*Then Jesus said to his disciples, "I tell you the truth, it is hard for a rich man to enter the kingdom of heaven."*

## Luke 12:21, 33

*"This is how it will be with anyone who stores up things for himself but is not rich toward God. Sell your possessions and give to the poor. Provide purses for yourselves that will not wear out, a treasure in heaven that will not be exhausted, where no thief comes near and no moth destroys."*

# Honesty

### Deuteronomy 25:14–15

*Do not have two differing measures in your house—one large, one small. You must have accurate and honest weights and measures, so that you may live long in the land the Lord your God is giving you.*

### Psalm 112:1–3, 5

*Praise the Lord. Blessed is the man who fears the Lord, who finds great delight in his commands. His children will be mighty in the land; the generation of the upright will be blessed. Wealth and riches are in his house, and his righteousness endures forever. Good will come to him who is generous and lends freely, who conducts his affairs with justice.*

### Proverbs 10:3, 9

*The Lord does not let the righteous go hungry but he thwarts the craving of the wicked. The man of integrity walks securely, but he who takes crooked paths will be found out.*

### Proverbs 13:5, 11, 21

*The righteous hate what is false, but the wicked bring shame and disgrace. Dishonest money dwindles away, but he who gathers money little by little makes it grow.*

*Misfortune pursues the sinner, but prosperity is the reward of the righteous.*

## Proverbs 16:8

*Better a little with righteousness than much gain with injustice.*

## Proverbs 20:7

*The righteous man leads a blameless life; blessed are his children after him.*

## Proverbs 24:27

*Finish your outdoor work and get your fields ready; after that, build your house.*

## Proverbs 27:1

*Do not boast about tomorrow, for you do not know what a day may bring forth.*

## Proverbs 28:18

*He whose walk is blameless is kept safe, but he whose ways are perverse will suddenly fall.*

**Proverbs 30:7–8**

*Two things I ask of you, O Lord; do not refuse me before I die: Keep falsehood and lies far from me; give me neither poverty nor riches, but give me only my daily bread.*

# Honesty Versus Unmerited Gain

**Deuteronomy 25:15**

*You must have accurate and honest weights and measures, so that you may live long in the land the Lord your God is giving you.*

**Proverbs 11:1**

*The Lord abhors dishonest scales, but accurate weights are his delight.*

**Proverbs 16:8**

*Better a little with righteousness than much gain with injustice.*

**Proverbs 22:16**

*He who oppresses the poor to increase his wealth and he who gives gifts to the rich—both come to poverty.*

**Proverbs 28:8**

*He who increases his wealth by exorbitant interest amasses it for another, who will be kind to the poor.*

**Jeremiah 22:13**

*Woe to him who builds his palace by unrighteousness, his upper rooms by injustice, making his countrymen work for nothing, not paying them for their labor.*

**Luke 16:10**

*Whoever can be trusted with very little can also be trusted with much, and whoever is dishonest with very little will also be dishonest with much.*

**Romans 12:17**

*Do not repay anyone evil for evil. Be careful to do what is right in the eyes of everybody.*

# Humility

**Proverbs 22:4**

*Humility and the fear of the Lord bring wealth and honor and life.*

## Jeremiah 9:24

*"But let him who boasts boast about this: that he under-stands and knows me, that I am the Lord, who exercises kindness, justice and righteousness on earth, for in these I delight," declares the Lord.*

## Matthew 6:1–3

*"Be careful not to do your 'acts of righteousness' before men, to be seen by them. If you do, you will have no reward from your Father in heaven.*

*"So when you give to the needy, do not announce it with trumpets, as the hypocrites do in the synagogues and on the streets, to be honored by men. I tell you the truth, they have received their reward in full. But when you give to the needy, do not let your left hand know what your right hand is doing."*

## Luke 17:3

*"So watch yourselves. If your brother sins, rebuke him, and if he repents, forgive him."*

## Luke 19:8

*But Zacchaeus stood up and said to the Lord, "Look, Lord! Here and now I give half of my possessions to the poor, and if I have cheated anybody out of anything, I will pay back four times the amount."*

## 1 Corinthians 1:26–31

*Brothers, think of what you were when you were called. Not many of you were wise by human standards; not many were influential; not many were of noble birth. But God chose the foolish things of the world to shame the wise; God chose the weak things of the world to shame the strong. He chose the lowly things of this world and the despised things-and the things that are not—to nullify the things that are, so that no one may boast before him. It is because of him that you are in Christ Jesus, who has become for us wisdom from God—that is, our righteousness, holiness and redemption. Therefore, as it is written: "Let him who boasts boast in the Lord."*

# Inheritance

## Proverbs 13:22

*A good man leaves an inheritance for his children's children, but a sinner's wealth is stored up for the righteous.*

## Proverbs 17:2

*A wise servant will rule over a disgraceful son, and will share the inheritance as one of the brothers.*

## Proverbs 20:21

*An inheritance quickly gained at the beginning will not be blessed at the end.*

## Ecclesiastes 2:18–19, 21

*I hated all the things I had toiled for under the sun, because I must leave them to the one who comes after me. And who knows whether he will be a wise man or a fool? Yet he will have control over all the work into which I have poured my effort and skill under the sun. This too is meaningless. For a man may do his work with wisdom, knowledge and skill, and then he must leave all he owns to someone who has not worked for it. This too is meaningless and a great misfortune.*

## Ezekiel 46:16–18

*This is what the Sovereign Lord says: "If the prince makes a gift from his inheritance to one of his sons, it will also belong to his descendants; it is to be their property by inheritance. If, however, he makes a gift from his inheritance to one of his servants, the servant may keep it until the year of freedom; then it will revert to the prince. His inheritance belongs to his sons only; it is theirs. The prince must not take any of the inheritance of the people, driving them off their property. He is to give his sons their inheritance out of his own property, so that none of my people will be separated from his property."*

## Luke 15:11–31

*Jesus continued: "There was a man who had two sons. The younger one said to his father, 'Father, give me my share of the estate.' So he divided his property between them.*

*"Not long after that, the younger son got together all he had, set off for a distant country and there squandered his wealth in wild living. After he had spent everything, there was a severe famine in that whole country, and he began to be in need. So he went and hired himself out to a citizen of that country, who sent him to his fields to feed pigs. He longed to fill his stomach with the pods that the pigs were eating, but no one gave him anything.*

*"When he came to his senses, he said, 'How many of my father's hired men have food to spare, and here I am starving to death! I will set out and go back to my father and say to him: Father, I have sinned against heaven and against you. I am no longer worthy to be called your son; make me like one of your hired men.' So he got up and went to his father.*

*"But while he was still a long way off, his father saw him and was filled with compassion for him; he ran to his son, threw his arms around him and kissed him.*

*"The son said to him, 'Father, I have sinned against heaven and against you. I am no longer worthy to be called your son.'*

*"But the father said to his servants, 'Quick! Bring the best robe and put it on him. Put a ring on his finger and sandals on his feet. Bring the fattened calf and kill it. Let's have a feast and celebrate. For this son of mine was dead and is alive again; he was lost and is found.' So they began to celebrate.*

*"Meanwhile, the older son was in the field. When he came near the house, he heard music and dancing. So he called one of the servants and asked him what was going on. 'Your brother has come,' he replied, 'and your father has killed the fattened calf because he has him back safe and sound.'*

*"The older brother became angry and refused to go in. So his father went out and pleaded with him. But he answered his father, 'Look! All these years I've been slaving for you and never disobeyed your orders. Yet you never gave me even a young goat so I could celebrate with my friends. But when this son of yours who has squandered your property with prostitutes comes home, you kill the fattened calf for him!'*

*"'My son,' the father said, 'you are always with me, and everything I have is yours.'"*

# Investing

### Psalm 62:10

*Do not trust in extortion or take pride in stolen goods; though your riches increase, do not set your heart on them.*

### Proverbs 11:24, 28

*One man gives freely, yet gains even more; another withholds unduly, but comes to poverty. Whoever trusts in his riches will fall, but the righteous will thrive like a green leaf.*

### Proverbs 16:1–9

*To man belong the plans of the heart, but from the Lord comes the reply of the tongue. All a man's ways seem innocent to him, but motives are weighed by the Lord. Commit to the Lord whatever you do, and your plans will succeed. The Lord works out everything for his own ends—even the wicked for a day of disaster. The Lord detests all the proud of heart. Be sure of this: They will not go unpunished. Through love and faithfulness sin is atoned for; through the fear of the Lord a man avoids evil. When a man's ways are pleasing to the Lord, he makes even his enemies live at peace with him. Better a little with righteousness than much gain with injustice. In his heart a man plans his course, but the Lord determines his steps.*

**Proverbs 21:5**

*The plans of the diligent lead to profit as surely as haste leads to poverty.*

**Proverbs 23:4–5**

*Do not wear yourself out to get rich; have the wisdom to show restraint. Cast but a glance at riches, and they are gone, for they will surely sprout wings and fly off to the sky like an eagle.*

# Investments

**Proverbs 21:20**

*In the house of the wise are stores of choice food and oil, but a foolish man devours all he has.*

**Proverbs 24:27**

*Finish your outdoor work and get your fields ready; after that, build your house.*

**Ecclesiastes 6:3**

*A man may have a hundred children and live many years; yet no matter how long he lives, if he cannot enjoy his prosperity and does not receive proper burial, I say that a stillborn child is better off than he.*

## Matthew 6:19–21

*"Do not store up for yourselves treasures on earth, where moth and rust destroy, and where thieves break in and steal. But store up for yourselves treasures in heaven, where moth and rust do not destroy, and where thieves do not break in and steal. For where your treasure is, there your heart will be also."*

## Matthew 13:22

*"The one who received the seed that fell among the thorns is the man who hears the word, but the worries of this life and the deceitfulness of wealth choke it, making it unfruitful."*

## Matthew 25:14–30, 45

*"Again, it will be like a man going on a journey, who called his servants and entrusted his property to them. To one he gave five talents of money, to another two talents, and to another one talent, each according to his ability. Then he went on his journey. The man who had received the five talents went at once and put his money to work and gained five more. So also, the one with the two talents gained two more. But the man who had received the one talent went off, dug a hole in the ground and hid his master's money.*

*"After a long time the master of those servants returned and settled accounts with them. The man who had received the five talents brought the other five. 'Master,' he said, 'you entrusted me with five talents. See, I have gained five more.'*

*"His master replied, 'Well done, good and faithful servant! You have been faithful with a few things; I will put you in charge of many things. Come and share your master's happiness!'*

*"The man with the two talents also came. 'Master,' he said, 'you entrusted me with two talents; see, I have gained two more.'*

*"His master replied, 'Well done, good and faithful servant! You have been faithful with a few things; I will put you in charge of many things. Come and share your master's happiness!'*

*"Then the man who had received the one talent came. 'Master,' he said, 'I knew that you are a hard man, harvesting where you have not sown and gathering where you have not scattered seed. So I was afraid and went out and hid your talent in the ground. See, here is what belongs to you.'*

*"His master replied, 'You wicked, lazy servant! So you knew that I harvest where I have not sown and gather where I have not scattered seed? Well then, you should*

*have put my money on deposit with the bankers, so that when I returned I would have received it back with interest.*

*"'Take the talent from him and give it to the one who has the ten talents. For everyone who has will be given more, and he will have an abundance. Whoever does not have, even what he has will be taken from him. And throw that worthless servant outside, into the darkness, where there will be weeping and gnashing of teeth.' He will reply, 'I tell you the truth, whatever you did not do for one of the least of these, you did not do for me.'"*

## Luke 14:28–29

*"Suppose one of you wants to build a tower. Will he not first sit down and estimate the cost to see if he has enough money to complete it? For if he lays the foundation and is not able to finish it, everyone who sees it will ridicule him."*

## Luke 19:13–26

*"So he called ten of his servants and gave them ten minas. 'Put this money to work,' he said, 'until I come back.'*

*"But his subjects hated him and sent a delegation after him to say, 'We don't want this man to be our king.'*

*"He was made king, however, and returned home. Then he sent for the servants to whom he had given the money, in order to find out what they had gained with it.*

*"The first one came and said, 'Sir, your mina has earned ten more.'*

*"'Well done, my good servant!' his master replied. 'Because you have been trustworthy in a very small matter, take charge of ten cities.'*

*"The second came and said, 'Sir, your mina has earned five more.'*

*"His master answered, 'You take charge of five cities.'*

*"Then another servant came and said, 'Sir, here is your mina; I have kept it laid away in a piece of cloth. I was afraid of you, because you are a hard man. You take out what you did not put in and reap what you did not sow.'*

*"His master replied, 'I will judge you by your own words, you wicked servant! You knew, did you, that I am a hard man, taking out what I did not put in, and reaping what I did not sow? Why then didn't you put my money on deposit, so that when I came back, I could have collected it with interest?'*

*"Then he said to those standing by, 'Take his mina away from him and give it to the one who has ten minas.'*

*"'Sir,' they said, 'he already has ten!'*

*"He replied, 'I tell you that to everyone who has, more will be given, but as for the one who has nothing, even what he has will be taken away.'"*

**2 Peter 2:20**

*If they have escaped the corruption of the world by knowing our Lord and Savior Jesus Christ and are again entangled in it and overcome, they are worse off at the end than they were at the beginning.*

**2 Peter 3:10**

*But the day of the Lord will come like a thief. The heavens will disappear with a roar; the elements will be destroyed by fire, and the earth and everything in it will be laid bare.*

## Laziness

**Proverbs 6:6–11**

*Go to the ant, you sluggard; consider its ways and be wise! It has no commander, no overseer or ruler, yet it stores its provisions in summer and gathers its food at harvest. How long will you lie there, you sluggard? When will you get up from your sleep? A little sleep, a little slumber, a little folding of the hands to rest—and poverty will come on you like a bandit and scarcity like an armed man.*

**Proverbs 12:24**

*Diligent hands will rule, but laziness ends in slave labor.*

**Proverbs 13:11**

*Dishonest money dwindles away, but he who gathers money little by little makes it grow.*

**Proverbs 14:4**

*Where there are no oxen, the manger is empty, but from the strength of an ox comes an abundant harvest.*

**Proverbs 19:15**

*Laziness brings on deep sleep, and the shiftless man goes hungry.*

**Proverbs 21:17**

*He who loves pleasure will become poor; whoever loves wine and oil will never be rich.*

**Proverbs 22:13**

*The sluggard says, "There is a lion outside!" or, "I will be murdered in the streets!"*

**Proverbs 26:13**

*The sluggard says, "There is a lion in the road, a fierce lion roaming the streets!"*

**2 Thessalonians 3:6, 10**

*In the name of the Lord Jesus Christ, we command you, brothers, to keep away from every brother who is idle and does not live according to the teaching you received from us. For even when we were with you, we gave you this rule: "If a man will not work, he shall not eat."*

# Lending

**Exodus 22:25–26**

*If you lend money to one of my people among you who is needy, do not be like a moneylender; charge him no interest. If you take your neighbor's cloak as a pledge, return it to him by sunset.*

## Deuteronomy 23:19–20

*Do not charge your brother interest, whether on money or food or anything else that may earn interest. You may charge a foreigner interest, but not a brother Israelite, so that the Lord your God may bless you in everything you put your hand to in the land you are entering to possess.*

## Deuteronomy 24:10–11

*When you make a loan of any kind to your neighbor, do not go into his house to get what he is offering as a pledge. Stay outside and let the man to whom you are making the loan bring the pledge out to you.*

## Nehemiah 5:7, 10

*I pondered them in my mind and then accused the nobles and officials. I told them, "You are exacting usury from your own countrymen!" So I called together a large meeting to deal with them. I and my brothers and my men are also lending the people money and grain. But let the exacting of usury stop!*

**Psalm 15:5**

*Who lends his money without usury and does not accept a bribe against the innocent. He who does these things will never be shaken.*

**Psalm 37:26**

*They are always generous and lend freely; their children will be blessed.*

**Proverbs 28:8**

*He who increases his wealth by exorbitant interest amasses it for another, who will be kind to the poor.*

**Ezekiel 18:8**

*He does not lend at usury or take excessive interest. He withholds his hand from doing wrong and judges fairly between man and man.*

**Luke 6:34–35**

*"And if you lend to those from whom you expect repayment, what credit is that to you? Even 'sinners' lend to 'sinners,' expecting to be repaid in full. But love your enemies, do good to them, and lend to them without expecting to get anything back. Then your reward will be great, and you will be sons of the Most High, because he is kind to the ungrateful and wicked."*

**Luke 7:41**

*"Two men owed money to a certain moneylender. One owed him five hundred denarii, and the other fifty."*

# Needs

**Psalm 37:25**

*I was young and now I am old, yet I have never seen the righteous forsaken or their children begging bread.*

**Matthew 6:8, 25–33**

*"Do not be like them, for your Father knows what you need before you ask him.*

*"Therefore I tell you, do not worry about your life, what you will eat or drink; or about your body, what you will wear. Is not life more important than food, and the body more important than clothes? Look at the birds of the air; they do not sow or reap or store away in barns, and yet your heavenly Father feeds them. Are you not much more valuable than they? Who of you by worrying can add a single hour to his life?*

*"And why do you worry about clothes? See how the lilies of the field grow. They do not labor or spin. Yet I tell you that not even Solomon in all his splendor was dressed*

*like one of these. If that is how God clothes the grass of the field, which is here today and tomorrow is thrown into the fire, will he not much more clothe you, O you of little faith? So do not worry, saying, 'What shall we eat?' or 'What shall we drink?' or 'What shall we wear?' For the pagans run after all these things, and your heavenly Father knows that you need them. But seek first his kingdom and his righteousness, and all these things will be given to you as well."*

**Philippians 4:19**

*And my God will meet all your needs according to his glorious riches in Christ Jesus.*

# Planning

**Proverbs 16:1**

*To man belong the plans of the heart, but from the Lord comes the reply of the tongue.*

# Prosperity

**Genesis 39:3**

*When his master saw that the Lord was with him and that the Lord gave him success in everything he did.*

**Deuteronomy 28:11**

*The Lord will grant you abundant prosperity—in the fruit of your womb, the young of your livestock and the crops of your ground—in the land he swore to your forefathers to give you.*

**Deuteronomy 29:9**

*Carefully follow the terms of this covenant, so that you may prosper in everything you do.*

**2 Chronicles 31:21**

*In everything that he undertook in the service of God's temple and in obedience to the law and the commands, he sought his God and worked wholeheartedly. And so he prospered.*

**Psalm 1:3**

*He is like a tree planted by streams of water, which yields its fruit in season and whose leaf does not wither. Whatever he does prospers.*

**Psalm 35:27**

*May those who delight in my vindication shout for joy and gladness; may they always say, "The Lord be exalted, who delights in the well-being of his servant."*

**Luke 15:13**

*"Not long after that, the younger son got together all he had, set off for a distant country and there squandered his wealth in wild living."*

**John 6:12**

*When they had all had enough to eat, he said to his disciples, "Gather the pieces that are left over. Let nothing be wasted."*

## Retirement

**Psalm 37:25**

*I was young and now I am old, yet I have never seen the righteous forsaken or their children begging bread.*

**Proverbs 16:31**

*Gray hair is a crown of splendor; it is attained by a righteous life.*

**Proverbs 20:29**

*The glory of young men is their strength, gray hair the splendor of the old.*

# Saving

### Proverbs 6:6–8

*Go to the ant, you sluggard; consider its ways and be wise! It has no commander, no overseer or ruler, yet it stores its provisions in summer and gathers its food at harvest.*

### Proverbs 21:20

*In the house of the wise are stores of choice food and oil, but a foolish man devours all he has.*

### Proverbs 30:24–25

*Four things on earth are small, yet they are extremely wise: Ants are creatures of little strength, yet they store up their food in the summer;*

# Sharing

### Exodus 16:18–20

*And when they measured it by the omer, he who gathered much did not have too much, and he who gathered little did not have too little. Each one gathered as much as he needed. Then Moses said to them, "No one is to keep any of it until morning." However, some of them paid no attention to Moses; they kept part of it until morning, but it was full of maggots and began to smell. So Moses was angry with them.*

### Acts 4:32

*All the believers were one in heart and mind. No one claimed that any of his possessions was his own, but they shared everything they had.*

### Romans 12:13

*Share with God's people who are in need. Practice hospitality.*

### 1 Corinthians 9:7–11, 14

*Who serves as a soldier at his own expense? Who plants a vineyard and does not eat of its grapes? Who tends a flock and does not drink of the milk? Do I say this merely from a human point of view? Doesn't the Law say the same thing? For it is written in the Law of Moses: "Do not muzzle an ox while it is treading out the grain." Is it about oxen that God is concerned? Surely he says this for us, doesn't he? Yes, this was written for us, because when the plowman plows and the thresher threshes, they ought to do so in the hope of sharing in the harvest. If we have sown spiritual seed among you, is it too much if we reap a material harvest from you? In the same way, the Lord has commanded that those who preach the gospel should receive their living from the gospel.*

## 2 Corinthians 8:8–15

*I am not commanding you, but I want to test the sincerity of your love by comparing it with the earnestness of others. For you know the grace of our Lord Jesus Christ, that though he was rich, yet for your sakes he became poor, so that you through his poverty might become rich. And here is my advice about what is best for you in this matter: Last year you were the first not only to give but also to have the desire to do so. Now finish the work, so that your eager willingness to do it may be matched by your completion of it, according to your means. For if the willingness is there, the gift is acceptable according to what one has, not according to what he does not have. Our desire is not that others might be relieved while you are hard pressed, but that there might be equality. At the present time your plenty will supply what they need, so that in turn their plenty will supply what you need. Then there will be equality, as it is written: "He who gathered much did not have too much, and he who gathered little did not have too little."*

## 2 Corinthians 9:6–13

*Remember this: Whoever sows sparingly will also reap sparingly, and whoever sows generously will also reap generously. Each man should give what he has decided in his heart to give, not reluctantly or under compulsion, for God loves a cheerful giver. And God is able to make all grace abound to you, so that in all things at all times, having all that you need, you will abound in every good work. As it is written: "He has scattered abroad his gifts to the poor; his righteousness endures forever." Now he who supplies seed to the sower and bread for food will also supply and increase your store of seed and will enlarge the harvest of your righteousness. You will be made rich in every way so that you can be generous on every occasion, and through us your generosity will result in thanksgiving to God. This service that you perform is not only supplying the needs of God's people but is also overflowing in many expressions of thanks to God. Because of the service by which you have proved yourselves, men will praise God for the obedience that accompanies your confession of the gospel of Christ, and for your generosity in sharing with them and with everyone else.*

**Galatians 6:6**

*Anyone who receives instruction in the word must share all good things with his instructor.*

## Self-Control

**Matthew 7:13–14**

*Enter through the narrow gate. For wide is the gate and broad is the road that leads to destruction, and many enter through it. But small is the gate and narrow the road that leads to life, and only a few find it.*

**2 Corinthians 8:11**

*Now finish the work, so that your eager willingness to do it may be matched by your completion of it, according to your means.*

**Hebrews 12:11**

*No discipline seems pleasant at the time, but painful. Later on, however, it produces a harvest of righteousness and peace for those who have been trained by it.*

# Slothfulness

**Proverbs 18:9**

*One who is slack in his work is brother to one who destroys.*

**Proverbs 24:30–31**

*I went past the field of the sluggard, past the vineyard of the man who lacks judgment; thorns had come up everywhere, the ground was covered with weeds, and the stone wall was in ruins.*

**Ecclesiastes 10:18**

*If a man is lazy, the rafters sag; if his hands are idle, the house leaks.*

**2 Thessalonians 3:11**

*We hear that some among you are idle. They are not busy; they are busybodies.*

**Hebrews 6:12**

*We do not want you to become lazy, but to imitate those who through faith and patience inherit what has been promised.*

## Speculation

**Ecclesiastes 5:15–17**

*Naked a man comes from his mother's womb, and as he comes, so he departs. He takes nothing from his labor that he can carry in his hand. This too is a grievous evil: As a man comes, so he departs, and what does he gain, since he toils for the wind? All his days he eats in darkness, with great frustration, affliction and anger.*

# Suing

### Matthew 5:42

*"Give to the one who asks you, and do not turn away from the one who wants to borrow from you."*

### Matthew 6:3

*"But when you give to the needy, do not let your left hand know what your right hand is doing."*

### Matthew 10:42

*"And if anyone gives even a cup of cold water to one of these little ones because he is my disciple, I tell you the truth, he will certainly not lose his reward."*

### Matthew 13:12

*"Whoever has will be given more, and he will have an abundance. Whoever does not have, even what he has will be taken from him."*

### Luke 6:30–36

*"Give to everyone who asks you, and if anyone takes what belongs to you, do not demand it back. Do to others as you would have them do to you. "If you love those who love you, what credit is that to you? Even 'sinners'*

*love those who love them. And if you do good to those who are good to you, what credit is that to you? Even 'sinners' do that. And if you lend to those from whom you expect repayment, what credit is that to you? Even 'sinners' lend to 'sinners,' expecting to be repaid in full. But love your enemies, do good to them, and lend to them without expecting to get anything back. Then your reward will be great, and you will be sons of the Most High, because he is kind to the ungrateful and wicked. Be merciful, just as your Father is merciful."*

## Luke 12:57–58

*"Why don't you judge for yourselves what is right? As you are going with your adversary to the magistrate, try hard to be reconciled to him on the way, or he may drag you off to the judge, and the judge turn you over to the officer, and the officer throw you into prison."*

## 1 Corinthians 6:1–7

*If any of you has a dispute with another, dare he take it before the ungodly for judgment instead of before the saints? Do you not know that the saints will judge the world? And if you are to judge the world, are you not competent to judge trivial cases? Do you not know that we will judge angels? How much more the things of this life! Therefore, if you have disputes about such matters, appoint as judges even men of little account in the church! I say this to shame you. Is it possible that there is nobody among you wise enough to judge a dispute between believers? But instead, one brother goes to law against another-and this in front of unbelievers! The very fact that you have lawsuits among you means you have been completely defeated already. Why not rather be wronged? Why not rather be cheated?*

## Supporting the Wealthy

**Deuteronomy 1:17**

*Do not show partiality in judging; hear both small and great alike. Do not be afraid of any man, for judgment belongs to God. Bring me any case too hard for you, and I will hear it.*

**Deuteronomy 16:19**

*Do not pervert justice or show partiality. Do not accept a bribe, for a bribe blinds the eyes of the wise and twists the words of the righteous.*

**Proverbs 14:20**

*But any winged creature that is clean you may eat.*

**Proverbs 28:21**

*To show partiality is not good—yet a man will do wrong for a piece of bread.*

## Taxes

### Matthew 17:24–27

*After Jesus and his disciples arrived in Capernaum, the collectors of the two-drachma tax came to Peter and asked, "Doesn't your teacher pay the temple tax?"*

*"Yes, he does," he replied.*

*When Peter came into the house, Jesus was the first to speak. "What do you think, Simon?" he asked. "From whom do the kings of the earth collect duty and taxes—from their own sons or from others?"*

*"From others," Peter answered. "Then the sons are exempt," Jesus said to him. "But so that we may not offend them, go to the lake and throw out your line. Take the first fish you catch; open its mouth and you will find a four-drachma coin. Take it and give it to them for my tax and yours."*

### Mark 12:14–17

*They came to him and said, "Teacher, we know you are a man of integrity. You aren't swayed by men, because you pay no attention to who they are; but you teach the way of God in accordance with the truth. Is it right to pay taxes to Caesar or not? Should we pay or shouldn't we?" But Jesus knew their hypocrisy. "Why are you try-*

*ing to trap me?" he asked. "Bring me a denarius and let me look at it." They brought the coin, and he asked them, "Whose portrait is this? And whose inscription?" "Caesar's," they replied. Then Jesus said to them, "Give to Caesar what is Caesar's and to God what is God's." And they were amazed at him.*

## Luke 20:22–25

*Is it right for us to pay taxes to Caesar or not?" He saw through their duplicity and said to them, "Show me a denarius. Whose portrait and inscription are on it?" "Caesar's," they replied. He said to them, "Then give to Caesar what is Caesar's, and to God what is God's."*

## Romans 13:6–7

*This is also why you pay taxes, for the authorities are God's servants, who give their full time to governing. Give everyone what you owe him: If you owe taxes, pay taxes; if revenue, then revenue; if respect, then respect; if honor, then honor.*

# Tithing

## Genesis 14:20, 22

*And blessed be God Most High, who delivered your enemies into your hand." Then Abram gave him a tenth of everything. But Abram said to the king of Sodom, "I have raised my hand to the Lord, God Most High, Creator of heaven and earth, and have taken an oath."*

## Malachi 3:10

*"Bring the whole tithe into the storehouse, that there may be food in my house. Test me in this," says the Lord Almighty, "and see if I will not throw open the floodgates of heaven and pour out so much blessing that you will not have room enough for it."*

## Matthew 23:23

*"Woe to you, teachers of the law and Pharisees, you hypocrites! You give a tenth of your spices-mint, dill and cummin. But you have neglected the more important matters of the law-justice, mercy and faithfulness. You should have practiced the latter, without neglecting the former."*

## Luke 11:42

*"Woe to you Pharisees, because you give God a tenth of your mint, rue and all other kinds of garden herbs, but you neglect justice and the love of God. You should have practiced the latter without leaving the former undone."*

## Hebrews 7:1–10

*This Melchizedek was king of Salem and priest of God Most High. He met Abraham returning from the defeat of the kings and blessed him, and Abraham gave him a tenth of everything. First, his name means "king of righteousness"; then also, "king of Salem" means "king of peace." Without father or mother, without genealogy, without beginning of days or end of life, like the Son of God he remains a priest forever. Just think how great he was: Even the patriarch Abraham gave him a tenth of the plunder! Now the law requires the descendants of Levi who become priests to collect a tenth from the people-that is, their brothers-even though their brothers are descended from Abraham. This man, however, did not trace his descent from Levi, yet he collected a tenth from Abraham and blessed him who had the promises. And without doubt the lesser person is blessed by the greater. In the one case, the tenth is collected by men who die; but in the other case, by him who is declared to be living. One might even say that Levi, who collects the tenth, paid the tenth through Abraham, because when Melchizedek met Abraham, Levi was still in the body of his ancestor.*

## Trust

### Jeremiah 17:7–8

*But blessed is the man who trusts in the Lord, whose confidence is in him.*

*He will be like a tree planted by the water that sends out its roots by the stream. It does not fear when heat comes;*

*its leaves are always green. It has no worries in a year of drought and never fails to bear fruit.*

### Mark 6:9

*Wear sandals but not an extra tunic.*

### Mark 8:34

*Then he called the crowd to him along with his disciples and said: "If anyone would come after me, he must deny himself and take up his cross and follow me."*

### Philippians 4:19

*And my God will meet all your needs according to his glorious riches in Christ Jesus.*

## Truthfulness

### Psalm 1:1–2

*Blessed is the man who does not walk in the counsel of the wicked or stand in the way of sinners or sit in the seat of mockers. But his delight is in the law of the Lord, and on his law he meditates day and night.*

### Psalm 37:37

*Consider the blameless, observe the upright; there is a future for the man of peace.*

**Psalm 112:6**

*Surely he will never be shaken; a righteous man will be remembered forever.*

**Proverbs 10:16**

*The wages of the righteous bring them life, but the income of the wicked brings them punishment.*

**Proverbs 11:4**

*Wealth is worthless in the day of wrath, but righteousness delivers from death.*

**Proverbs 12:12**

*The wicked desire the plunder of evil men, but the root of the righteous flourishes.*

**Proverbs 13:22**

*A good man leaves an inheritance for his children's children, but a sinner's wealth is stored up for the righteous.*

**Proverbs 16:8, 11**

*Better a little with righteousness than much gain with injustice. Honest scales and balances are from the Lord; all the weights in the bag are of his making.*

**Proverbs 19:1**

*Better a poor man whose walk is blameless than a fool whose lips are perverse.*

**Proverbs 21:3**

*To do what is right and just is more acceptable to the Lord than sacrifice.*

**Proverbs 22:1**

*A good name is more desirable than great riches; to be esteemed is better than silver or gold.*

**Proverbs 28:6, 13**

*Better a poor man whose walk is blameless than a rich man whose ways are perverse. He who conceals his sins does not prosper, but whoever confesses and renounces them finds mercy.*

**Matthew 7:20**

*"Thus, by their fruit you will recognize them."*

**Matthew 17:24**

*After Jesus and his disciples arrived in Capernaum, the collectors of the two-drachma tax came to Peter and asked, "Doesn't your teacher pay the temple tax?"*

## Luke 3:12–13

*Tax collectors also came to be baptized. "Teacher," they asked, "what should we do?" "Don't collect any more than you are required to," he told them.*

## Luke 8:15

*"But the seed on good soil stands for those with a noble and good heart, who hear the word, retain it, and by persevering produce a crop."*

## Luke 12:58

*"As you are going with your adversary to the magistrate, try hard to be reconciled to him on the way, or he may drag you off to the judge, and the judge turn you over to the officer, and the officer throw you into prison."*

## Romans 13:7

*Give everyone what you owe him: If you owe taxes, pay taxes; if revenue, then revenue; if respect, then respect; if honor, then honor.*

## Romans 13:9

*The commandments, "Do not commit adultery," "Do not murder," "Do not steal," "Do not covet," and whatever other commandment there may be, are summed up in this one rule: "Love your neighbor as yourself."*

### Galatians 6:9

*Let us not become weary in doing good, for at the proper time we will reap a harvest if we do not give up.*

# Waste

### Genesis 41:36

*This food should be held in reserve for the country, to be used during the seven years of famine that will come upon Egypt, so that the country may not be ruined by the famine.*

# Wealth

### Proverbs 10:22

*Hatred stirs up dissension, but love covers over all wrongs.*

### Proverbs 28:13

*He who conceals his sins does not prosper, but whoever confesses and renounces them finds mercy.*

### Jeremiah 17:8–10

*He will be like a tree planted by the water that sends out its roots by the stream. It does not fear when heat comes; its leaves are always green. It has no worries in a year of drought and never fails to bear fruit." The heart is deceitful above all things and beyond cure. Who can understand it? "I the Lord search the heart and examine the mind, to reward a man according to his conduct, according to what his deeds deserve."*

## Luke 6:38

*"Give, and it will be given to you. A good measure, pressed down, shaken together and running over, will be poured into your lap. For with the measure you use, it will be measured to you."*

## John 10:10

*"The thief comes only to steal and kill and destroy; I have come that they may have life, and have it to the full."*

## 2 Corinthians 8:9

*For you know the grace of our Lord Jesus Christ, that though he was rich, yet for your sakes he became poor, so that you through his poverty might become rich.*

## Philippians 4:19

*And my God will meet all your needs according to his glorious riches in Christ Jesus.*

# Wives

### Proverbs 31:10–31

*A wife of noble character who can find? She is worth
far more than rubies. Her husband has full confidence
in her and lacks nothing of value. She brings him good,
not harm, all the days of her life. She selects wool and
flax and works with eager hands. She is like the merchant ships, bringing her food from afar. She gets up
while it is still dark; she provides food for her family and
portions for her servant girls. She considers a field and
buys it; out of her earnings she plants a vineyard. She
sets about her work vigorously; her arms are strong for
her tasks. She sees that her trading is profitable, and her
lamp does not go out at night. In her hand she holds the
distaff and grasps the spindle with her fingers. She opens
her arms to the poor and extends her hands to the needy.
When it snows, she has no fear for her household; for
all of them are clothed in scarlet. She makes coverings
for her bed; she is clothed in fine linen and purple. Her
husband is respected at the city gate, where he takes his
seat among the elders of the land. She makes linen garments and sells them, and supplies the merchants with
sashes. She is clothed with strength and dignity; she can
laugh at the days to come. She speaks with wisdom, and
faithful instruction is on her tongue. She watches over
the affairs of her household and does not eat the bread of
idleness. Her children arise and call her blessed; her husband also, and he praises her: "Many women do noble
things, but you surpass them all." Charm is deceptive,
and beauty is fleeting; but a woman who fears the Lord
is to be praised. Give her the reward she has earned.*

# Work

### Deuteronomy 24:14–15

*Do not take advantage of a hired man who is poor and needy, whether he is a brother Israelite or an alien living in one of your towns. Pay him his wages each day before sunset, because he is poor and is counting on it. Otherwise he may cry to the Lord against you, and you will be guilty of sin.*

### Proverbs 6:6–10

*Go to the ant, you sluggard; consider its ways and be wise! It has no commander, no overseer or ruler, yet it stores its provisions in summer and gathers its food at harvest. How long will you lie there, you sluggard? When will you get up from your sleep? A little sleep, a little slumber, a little folding of the hands to rest.*

### Proverbs 10:4–5

*Lazy hands make a man poor, but diligent hands bring wealth. He who gathers crops in summer is a wise son, but he who sleeps during harvest is a disgraceful son.*

### Proverbs 12:11, 24

*He who works his land will have abundant food, but he who chases fantasies lacks judgment. Diligent hands will rule, but laziness ends in slave labor.*

### Proverbs 14:23

*All hard work brings a profit, but mere talk leads only to poverty.*

### Proverbs 16:26

*The laborer's appetite works for him; his hunger drives him on.*

### Proverbs 28:19

*He who works his land will have abundant food, but the one who chases fantasies will have his fill of poverty.*

### Ephesians 4:28

*He who has been stealing must steal no longer, but must work, doing something useful with his own hands, that he may have something to share with those in need.*

# Worry

### Psalm 50:14–15

*Sacrifice thank offerings to God, fulfill your vows to the Most High, and call upon me in the day of trouble; I will deliver you, and you will honor me.*

## Proverbs 12:25

*An anxious heart weighs a man down, but a kind word
cheers him up.*

## Matthew 6:27–34

*"Who of you by worrying can add a single hour to his
life? And why do you worry about clothes? See how the
lilies of the field grow. They do not labor or spin. Yet I
tell you that not even Solomon in all his splendor was
dressed like one of these. If that is how God clothes the
grass of the field, which is here today and tomorrow is
thrown into the fire, will he not much more clothe you,
O you of little faith? So do not worry, saying, 'What
shall we eat?' or 'What shall we drink?' or 'What shall
we wear?' For the pagans run after all these things, and
your heavenly Father knows that you need them. But
seek first his kingdom and his righteousness, and all
these things will be given to you as well. Therefore do not
worry about tomorrow, for tomorrow will worry about
itself. Each day has enough trouble of its own."*

## Philippians 4:6

*Do not be anxious about anything, but in everything,
by prayer and petition, with thanksgiving, present your
requests to God.*

### 1 John 4:18

*There is no fear in love. But perfect love drives out fear, because fear has to do with punishment. The one who fears is not made perfect in love.*

# Source Material

21 Unbreakable Laws of Success, Max Anders, Thomas Nelson, 1996

A Christian Guide to Prosperity; Fries & Taylor, California: Communications Research, 1984

A Look At Stewardship, Word Aflame Publications, 2001

American Savings Education Council (http://www.asec.org)

Anointed For Business, Ed Silvoso, Regal, 2002

Avoiding Common Financial Mistakes, Ron Blue, Navpress, 1991

Baker Encyclopedia of the Bible; Walter Elwell, Michigan: Baker Book House, 1988

Becoming The Best, Barry Popplewell, England: Gower Publishing Company Limited, 1988

Business Proverbs, Steve Marr, Fleming H. Revell, 2001

Cheapskate Monthly, Mary Hunt

Commentary on the Old Testament; Keil-Delitzsch, Michigan: Eerdmans Publishing, 1986

Crown Financial Ministries, various publications

Customers As Partners, Chip Bell, Texas: Berrett-Koehler Publishers, 1994

Cut Your Bills in Half; Pennsylvania: Rodale Press, Inc., 1989

Debt-Free Living, Larry Burkett, Dimensions, 2001

Die Broke, Stephen M. Pollan & Mark Levine, HarperBusiness, 1997

Double Your Profits, Bob Fifer, Virginia: Lincoln Hall Press, 1993

Eerdmans' Handbook to the Bible, Michigan: William B. Eerdmans Publishing Company, 1987

Eight Steps to Seven Figures, Charles B. Carlson, Double Day, 2000

Everyday Life in Bible Times; Washington DC: National Geographic Society, 1967

Financial Dominion, Norvel Hayes, Harrison House, 1986

Financial Freedom, Larry Burkett, Moody Press, 1991

Financial Freedom, Patrick Clements, VMI Publishers, 2003

Financial Peace, Dave Ramsey, Viking Press, 2003

Financial Self-Defense; Charles Givens, New York: Simon And Schuster, 1990

Flood Stage, Oral Roberts, 1981

Generous Living, Ron Blue, Zondervan, 1997

Get It All Done, Tony and Robbie Fanning, New York:Pennsylvania: Chilton Book, 1979

Getting Out of Debt, Howard Dayton, Tyndale House, 1986

Getting Out of Debt, Mary Stephenson, Fact Sheet 436, University of Maryland Cooperative Extension Service, 1988

Giving and Tithing, Larry Burkett, Moody Press, 1991

God's Plan For Giving, John MacArthur, Jr., Moody Press, 1985

God's Will is Prosperity, Gloria Copeland, Harrison House, 1978

Great People of the Bible and How They Lived; New York: Reader's Digest, 1974

How Others Can Help You Get Out of Debt; Esther M. Maddux, Circular 759-3,

How To Make A Business Plan That Works, Henderson, North Island Sound Limited, 1989

How To Manage Your Money, Larry Burkett, Moody Press, 1999

How to Personally Profit From the Laws of Success, Sterling Sill, NIFP, Inc., 1978

How to Plan for Your Retirement; New York: Corrigan & Kaufman, Longmeadow Press, 1985

Is God Your Source?, Oral Roberts, 1992

It's Not Luck, Eliyahu Goldratt, Great Barrington, MA: The North River Press, 1994

Jesus CEO, Laurie Beth Jones, Hyperion, 1995

John Avanzini Answers Your Questions About Biblical Economics, Harrison House, 1992

Living on Less and Liking It More, Maxine Hancock, Chicago, Illinois: Moody Press, 1976

Making It Happen; Charles Conn, New Jersey: Fleming H. Revell Company, 1981

Master Your Money Or It Will Master You, Arlo E. Moehlenpah, Doing Good Ministries, 1999

Master Your Money; Ron Blue, Tennessee: Thomas Nelson, Inc. 1986

Miracle of Seed Faith, Oral Roberts, 1970

Mississippi State University Extension Service

Money, Possessions, and Eternity, Randy Alcorn, Tyndale House, 2003

More Than Enough, David Ramsey, Penguin Putnam Inc, 2002

Moving the Hand of God, John Avanzini, Harrison House, 1990

Multiplication, Tommy Barnett, Creation House, 1997

NebFacts, Nebraska Cooperative Extension

New York Post

One Up On Wall Street; New York: Peter Lynch, Simon And Schuster, 1989

Personal Finances, Larry Burkett, Moody Press, 1991

Portable MBA in Finance and Accounting; Livingstone, Canada: John Wiley & Sons, Inc., 1992

Principle-Centered Leadership, Stephen R. Covey, New York: Summit Books, 1991

Principles of Financial Management, Kolb & DeMong, Texas: Business Publications, Inc., 1988

Rapid Debt Reduction Strategies, John Avanzini, HIS Publishing, 1990

Real Wealth, Wade Cook, Arizona: Regency Books, 1985

See You At The Top, Zig Ziglar, Louisianna: Pelican Publishing Company, 1977

Seed-Faith Commentary on the Holy Bible, Oral Roberts, Pinoak Publications, 1975

Sharkproof, Harvey Mackay, New York: HarperCollins Publishers, 1993

Smart Money, Ken and Daria Dolan, New York: Random House, Inc., 1988

Strong's Concordance, Tennessee: Crusade Bible Publishers, Inc.,

Success by Design, Peter Hirsch, Bethany House, 2002

Success is the Quality of your Journey, Jennifer James, New York: Newmarket Press, 1983

Swim with the Sharks Without Being Eaten Alive, Harvey Mackay, William Morrow , 1988

The Almighty and the Dollar; Jim McKeever, Oregon: Omega Publications, 1981

The Challenge, Robert Allen, New York: Simon And Schuster, 1987

The Family Financial Workbook, Larry Burkett, Moody Press, 2002

The Management Methods of Jesus, Bob Briner, Thomas Nelson, 1996

The Millionaire Next Door, Thomas Stanley & William Danko, Pocket Books, 1996

The Money Book for Kids, Nancy Burgeson, Troll Associates,1992

The Money Book for King's Kids; Harold E. Hill, New Jersey: Fleming H. Revell Company, 1984

The Seven Habits of Highly Effective People, Stephen Covey, New York: Simon And Schuster, 1989

The Wealthy Barber, David Chilton, California: Prima Publishing, 1991

Theological Wordbook of the Old Testament, Chicago, Illinois: Moody Press, 1981

Treasury of Courage and Confidence, Norman Vincent Peale, New York: Doubleday & Co., 1970

True Prosperity, Dick Iverson, Bible Temple Publishing, 1993

Trust God For Your Finances, Jack Hartman, Lamplight Publications, 1983

University of Georgia Cooperative Extension Service, 1985

Virginia Cooperative Extension

Webster's Unabridged Dictionary, Dorset & Baber, 1983

What Is an Entrepreneur; David Robinson, MA: Kogan Page Limited, 1990

Word Meanings in the New Testament, Ralph Earle, Michigan: Baker Book House, 1986

Word Pictures in the New Testament; Robertson, Michigan: Baker Book House, 1930

Word Studies in the New Testament; Vincent, New York: Charles Scribner's Sons, 1914

Worth

You Can Be Financially Free, George Fooshee, Jr., 1976, Fleming H. Revell Company.

Your Key to God's Bank, Rex Humbard, 1977

Your Money Counts, Howard, Dayton, Tyndale House, 1997

Your Money Management, MaryAnn Paynter, Circular 1271, University of Illinois Cooperative Extension Service, 1987.

Your Money Matters, Malcolm MacGregor, Bethany Fellowship, Inc., 1977

Your Road to Recovery, Oral Roberts, Oliver Nelson, 1986

# Comments On Sources

Over the years I have collected bits and pieces of interesting material, written notes on sermons I've heard, jotted down comments on financial articles I've read, and gathered a lot of great information. It is unfortunate that I didn't record the sources of all of these notes in my earlier years. I gratefully extend my appreciation to the many writers, authors, teachers and pastors from whose articles and sermons I have gleaned much insight.

*Rich Brott*

# Online Resources

American Savings Education Council (http://www.asec.org)

Bloomberg.com (http://www.bloomberg.com)

Bureau of the Public Debt Online (http://www.publicdebt.treas.gov)

BusinessWeek (http://www.businessweek.com)

Charles Schwab & Co., Inc. (http://www.schwab.com)

Consumer Federation of America (http://www.consumerfed.org)

Debt Advice.org (http://www.debtadvice.org)

Federal Reserve System  (http://www.federalreserve.gov)

Fidelity Investments (http://www.fidelity.com)

Financial Planning Association (http://www.fpanet.org)

Forbes (www.forbes.com)

Fortune Magazine (http://www.fortune.com)

Generous Giving (http://www.generousgiving.org/)

Investing for Your Future (http://www.investing.rutgers.edu)

Kiplinger Magazine (http://www.kiplinger.com/)

Money Magazine (http://money.cnn.com)

MorningStar (http://www.morningstar.com)

MSN Money (http://moneycentral.msn.com)

Muriel Siebert (http://www.siebertnet.com)

National Center on Education and the Economy (http://www.ncee.org)

National Foundation for Credit Counseling (http://www.nfcc.org)

Quicken (http://www.quicken.com)

Smart Money (http://www.smartmoney.com)

Social Security Online (http://www.ssa.gov)

Standard & Poor's (http://www2.standardandpoors.com)

The Dollar Stretcher, Gary Foreman, (http://www.stretcher.com)

The Vanguard Group (http://flagship.vanguard.com)

U.S. Securities and Exchange Commission (http://www.sec.gov)

Yahoo! Finance (http://finance.yahoo.com)

# Magazine Resources

Business Week
Consumer Reports
Forbes
Kiplinger's Personal Finance
Money
Smart Money
US News and World Report

# Newspaper Resources

Barrons
Investors Business Daily
USA Today
Wall Street Journal
Washington Times

# Additional Resources *by Rich Brott*

## www.RichBrott.com

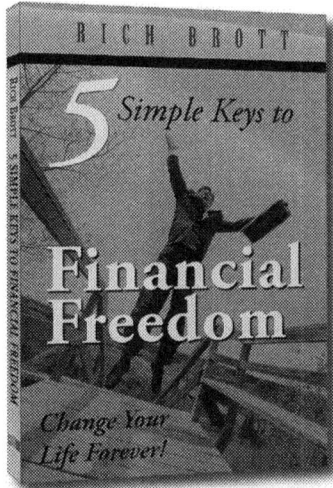

# 5 Simple Keys to Financial Freedom

*Change Your Life Forever!*

By Rich Brott

6" x 9", 108 pages
ISBN 1-60185-022-0
ISBN (EAN) 978-1-60185-022-5

a b c
**Book Publishing**

### Order online at:
www.RichBrott.com
www.amazon.com
www.barnesandnoble.com
www.booksamillion.com
www.citychristianpublishing.com
www.bordersstores.com

## www.AbcBookPublishing.com

# Additional Resources *by Rich Brott*

## www.RichBrott.com

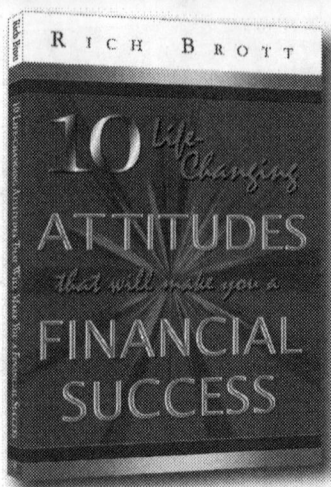

## 10 Life-Changing Attitudes
## That Will Make You
## a Financial Success

### By Rich Brott

6" x 9", 108 pages
ISBN 1-60185-021-2
ISBN (EAN) 978-1-60185-021-8

abc
**Book Publishing**

### *Order online at:*
www.RichBrott.com
www.amazon.com
www.barnesandnoble.com
www.booksamillion.com
www.citychristianpublishing.com
www.bordersstores.com

# www.AbcBookPublishing.com

# Additional Resources *by Rich Brott*

## www.RichBrott.com

**15 Biblical Responsibilities
Leading to Financial Wisdom**

*Accepting Personal Accountability*

By Rich Brott

6" x 9", 120 pages
ISBN 1-60185-010-7
ISBN (EAN) 978-1-60185-010-2

**Order online at:**
www.RichBrott.com
www.amazon.com
www.barnesandnoble.com
www.booksamillion.com
www.citychristianpublishing.com
www.bordersstores.com

abc
Book Publishing

# www.AbcBookPublishing.com

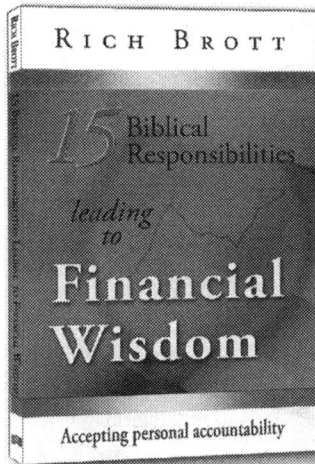

# Additional Resources *by Rich Brott*

## www.RichBrott.com

## 30 Biblical Principles for Managing Your Money

*Insights that Will Set You Free!*

By Rich Brott

6" x 9", 160 pages
ISBN 1-60185-012-3
ISBN (EAN) 978-1-60185-012-6

a b c
Book Publishing

### Order online at:

www.RichBrott.com
www.amazon.com
www.barnesandnoble.com
www.booksamillion.com
www.citychristianpublishing.com
www.bordersstores.com

## www.AbcBookPublishing.com

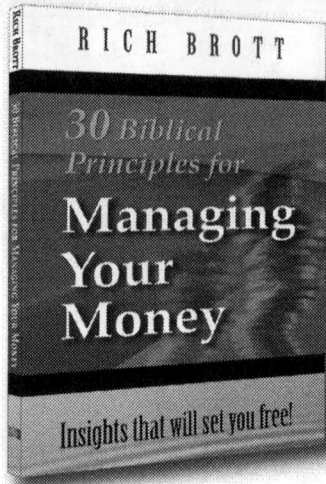

# Additional Resources *by Rich Brott*

## www.RichBrott.com

## 35 Keys to
## Financial Independence

*Finding the Freedom You Seek!*

### By Rich Brott

6" x 9", 176 pages
ISBN 1-60185-020-4
ISBN (EAN) 978-1-60185-020-1

a b c
**Book Publishing**

*Order online at:*
www.RichBrott.com
www.amazon.com
www.barnesandnoble.com
www.booksamillion.com
www.citychristianpublishing.com
www.bordersstores.com

## www.AbcBookPublishing.com

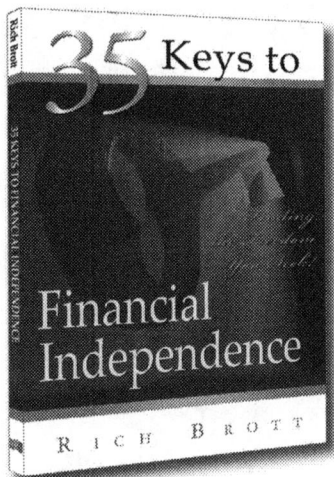

# Additional Resources *by Rich Brott*

## www.RichBrott.com

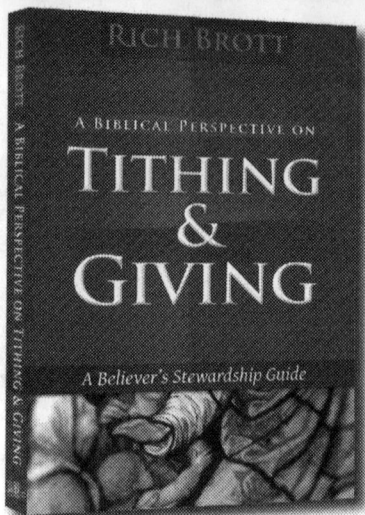

# A Biblical Perspective on Tithing & Giving

*A Believer's Stewardship Guide*

By Rich Brott

6" x 9", 172 pages
ISBN 1-60185-000-X
ISBN (EAN) 978-1-60185-000-3

abc
Book Publishing

**Order online at:**
www.RichBrott.com
www.amazon.com
www.barnesandnoble.com
www.booksamillion.com
www.citychristianpublishing.com
www.bordersstores.com

## www.AbcBookPublishing.com

# Additional Resources *by Rich Brott*

## www.RichBrott.com

## All the Financial Scriptures
## in the Bible with Commentary

### By Rich Brott

6" x 9", 364 pages
ISBN 1-60185-004-2
ISBN (EAN) 978-1-60185-004-1

a b c
**Book Publishing**

*Order online at:*
www.RichBrott.com
www.amazon.com
www.barnesandnoble.com
www.booksamillion.com
www.citychristianpublishing.com
www.bordersstores.com

## www.AbcBookPublishing.com

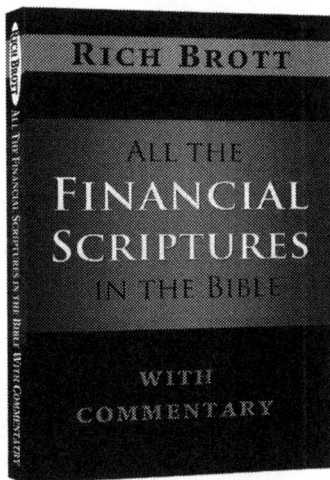

# Additional Resources *by Rich Brott*

## www.RichBrott.com

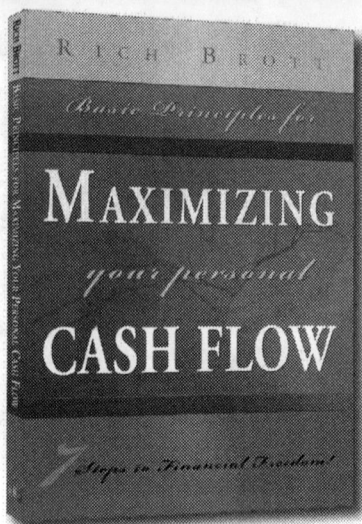

## Basic Principles for Maximizing
## Your Personal Cash Flow

*7 Steps to Financial Freedom!*

### By Rich Brott

6" x 9", 120 pages
ISBN 1-60185-019-0
ISBN (EAN) 978-1-60185-019-5

**abc**
Book Publishing

**Order online at:**
www.RichBrott.com
www.amazon.com
www.barnesandnoble.com
www.booksamillion.com
www.citychristianpublishing.com
www.bordersstores.com

## www.AbcBookPublishing.com

# Additional Resources *by Rich Brott*

## www.RichBrott.com

### Basic Principles of
### Conservative Investing

*9 Principles You Must Follow*

By Rich Brott

6" x 9", 116 pages
ISBN 1-60185-018-2
ISBN (EAN) 978-1-60185-018-8

abc
Book Publishing

*Order online at:*
www.RichBrott.com
www.amazon.com
www.barnesandnoble.com
www.booksamillion.com
www.citychristianpublishing.com
www.bordersstores.com

## www.AbcBookPublishing.com

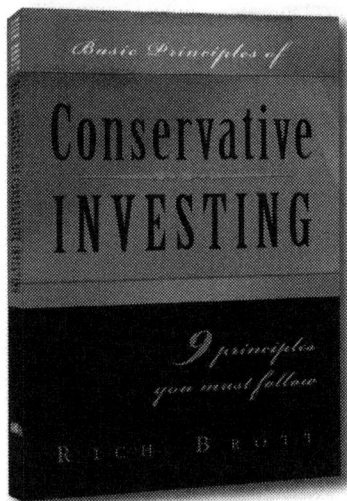

# Additional Resources *by Rich Brott*

## www.RichBrott.com

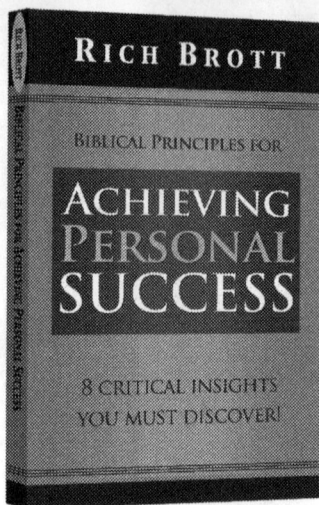

## Biblical Principles for
## Achieving Personal Success

*8 Critical Insights You Must Discover!*

By Rich Brott

6" x 9", 248 pages
ISBN 1-60185-013-1
ISBN (EAN) 978-1-60185-013-3

**abc**
Book Publishing

*Order online at:*
www.RichBrott.com
www.amazon.com
www.barnesandnoble.com
www.booksamillion.com
www.citychristianpublishing.com
www.bordersstores.com

## www.AbcBookPublishing.com

# Additional Resources *by Rich Brott*

## www.RichBrott.com

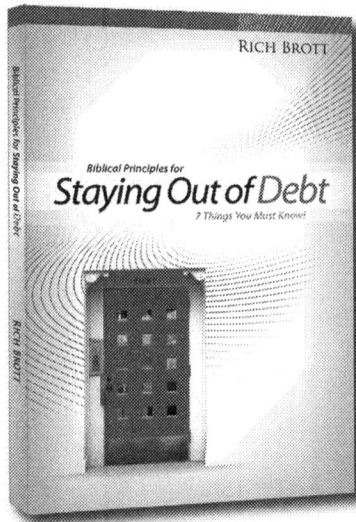

# Biblical Principles for Staying Out of Debt

*7 Things You Must Know!*

By Rich Brott

6" x 9", 120 pages
ISBN 1-60185-009-3
ISBN (EAN) 978-1-60185-009-6

abc
Book Publishing

### Order online at:
www.RichBrott.com
www.amazon.com
www.barnesandnoble.com
www.booksamillion.com
www.citychristianpublishing.com
www.bordersstores.com

# www.AbcBookPublishing.com

# Additional Resources *by Rich Brott*

## www.RichBrott.com

**Biblical Principles for
Financial Success**

*Student Workbook*

By Rich Brott

7.5" x 9.25", 228 pages
ISBN 1-60185-016-6
ISBN (EAN) 978-1-60185-016-4

abc
Book Publishing

*Order online at:*
www.RichBrott.com
www.amazon.com
www.barnesandnoble.com
www.booksamillion.com
www.citychristianpublishing.com
www.bordersstores.com

## www.AbcBookPublishing.com

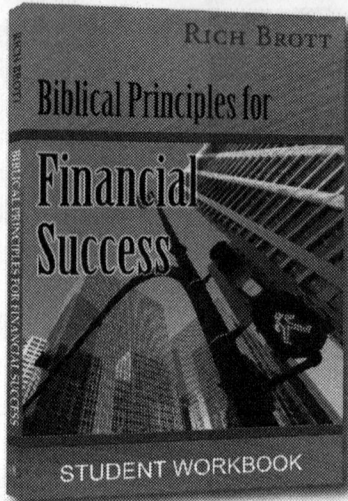

# Additional Resources *by Rich Brott*

## www.RichBrott.com

## Biblical Principles for Financial Success

*Teacher Workbook*

By Rich Brott

7.5" x 9.25", 228 pages
ISBN 1-60185-015-8
ISBN (EAN) 978-1-60185-015-7

a b c
**Book Publishing**

*Order online at:*
www.RichBrott.com
www.amazon.com
www.barnesandnoble.com
www.booksamillion.com
www.citychristianpublishing.com
www.bordersstores.com

## www.AbcBookPublishing.com

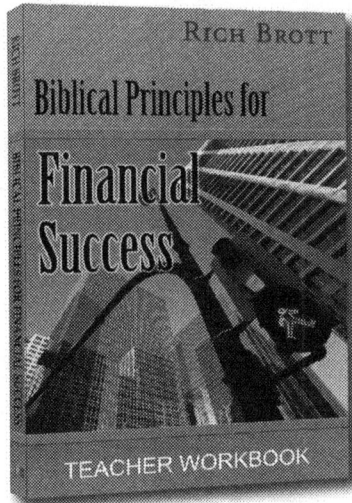

# Additional Resources *by Rich Brott*

## www.RichBrott.com

Biblical Principles that create

## SUCCESS
### through
## Productivity

How God Blesses
Our Work Ethic

## Biblical Principles that Create
## Success through Productivity

*How God Blesses Our Work Ethic*

### By Rich Brott

6" x 9", 224 pages
ISBN 1-60185-007-7
ISBN (EAN) 978-1-60185-007-2

abc
Book Publishing

*Order online at:*
www.RichBrott.com
www.amazon.com
www.barnesandnoble.com
www.booksamillion.com
www.citychristianpublishing.com
www.bordersstores.com

## www.AbcBookPublishing.com

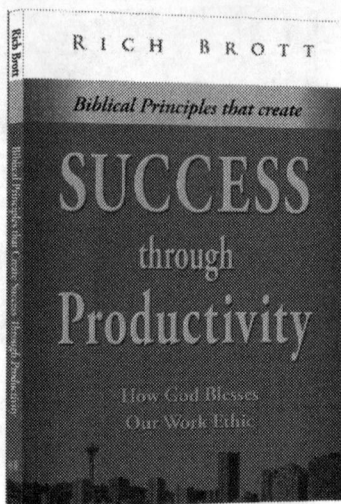

# Additional Resources *by Rich Brott*

## www.RichBrott.com

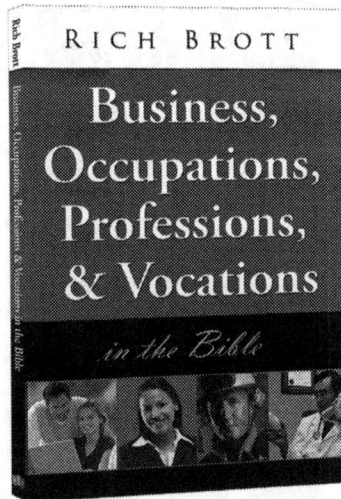

# Business, Occupations, Professions & Vocations in the Bible

## By Rich Brott

6" x 9", 212 pages
ISBN 1-60185-014-X
ISBN (EAN) 978-1-60185-014-0

**abc**
Book Publishing

### Order online at:
www.RichBrott.com
www.amazon.com
www.barnesandnoble.com
www.booksamillion.com
www.citychristianpublishing.com
www.bordersstores.com

## www.AbcBookPublishing.com

# Additional Resources *by Rich Brott*

## www.RichBrott.com

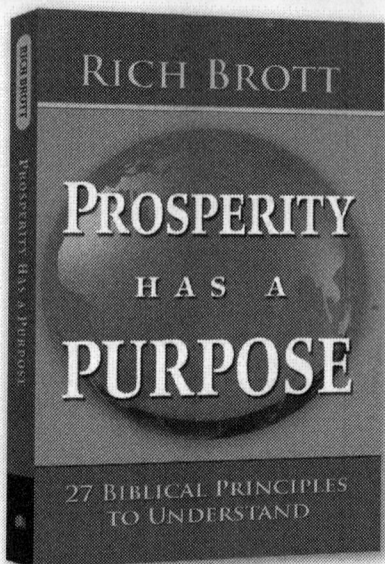

## Prosperity Has a Purpose!

*27 Biblical Principles to Understand*

By Rich Brott

6" x 9", 276 pages
ISBN 1-60185-006-9
ISBN (EAN) 978-1-60185-006-5

### abc
### Book Publishing

### Order online at:
www.RichBrott.com
www.amazon.com
www.barnesandnoble.com
www.booksamillion.com
www.citychristianpublishing.com
www.bordersstores.com

## www.AbcBookPublishing.com

# Additional Resources *by Rich Brott*

## www.RichBrott.com

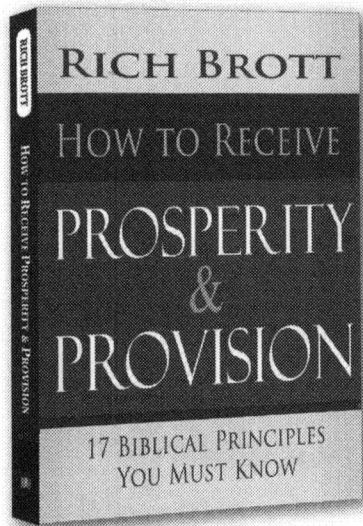

## How to Receive
## Prosperity & Provision

*17 Principles You Must Know*

### By Rich Brott

6" x 9", 296 pages
ISBN 1-60185-005-0
ISBN (EAN) 978-1-60185-005-8

a b c
**Book Publishing**

### *Order online at:*
www.RichBrott.com
www.amazon.com
www.barnesandnoble.com
www.booksamillion.com
www.citychristianpublishing.com
www.bordersstores.com

# www.AbcBookPublishing.com

# Additional Resources *by Rich Brott*

## www.RichBrott.com

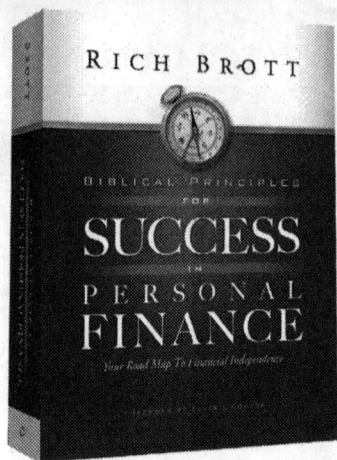

## Biblical Principles for
## Success in Personal Finance

*Your Roadmap to Financial Independence*

### By Rich Brott

7.5" x 10", 519 pages
ISBN 0-914936-72-7
ISBN (EAN) 978-0-914936-72-5

**abc Book Publishing**

### *Order online at:*

www.RichBrott.com
www.amazon.com
www.barnesandnoble.com
www.booksamillion.com
www.citychristianpublishing.com
www.bordersstores.com

## www.AbcBookPublishing.com

# Additional Resources *by Rich Brott*

## www.RichBrott.com

## Biblical Principles for Building a Successful Business

*A Practical Guide to Assessing, Evaluating, and Growing a Successful Cutting-Edge Enterprise in Today's Business Environment*

By Rich Brott & Frank Damazio

7.5" x 10", 477 pages
ISBN 1-59383-027-0
ISBN (EAN) 978-1-59383-027-4

abc
Book Publishing

*Order online at:*
www.RichBrott.com
www.amazon.com
www.barnesandnoble.com
www.booksamillion.com
www.citychristianpublishing.com
www.bordersstores.com

## www.AbcBookPublishing.com

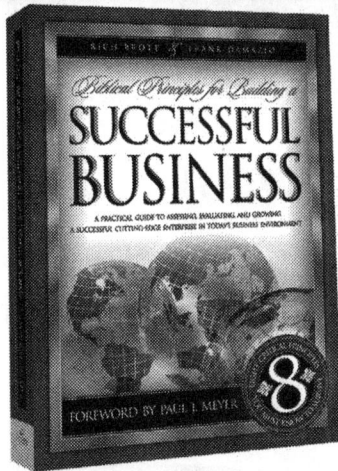

# Additional Resources *by Rich Brott*

## www.RichBrott.com

**RICH BROTT & FRANK DAMAZIO**

*Biblical Principles*
for becoming
# Debt Free!
RESCUE YOUR LIFE & LIBERATE YOUR FUTURE

5 Keys | 10 Attitudes | 15 Responsibilities
30 Biblical Principles | 35 Practical Applications

## Biblical Principles for Becoming Debt Free!

*Rescue Your Life and*
*Liberate Your Future!*

By Rich Brott & Frank Damazio

7.5" x 10", 320 pages
ISBN 1-886849-85-4
ISBN 978-1-886849-85-3

a b c
Book Publishing

### *Order online at:*
www.RichBrott.com
www.amazon.com
www.barnesandnoble.com
www.booksamillion.com
www.citychristianpublishing.com
www.bordersstores.com

## www.AbcBookPublishing.com

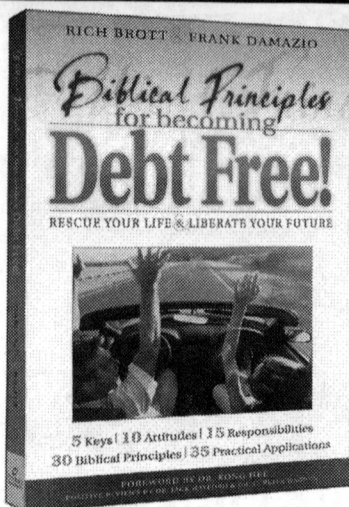

# Additional Resources *by Rich Brott*

## www.RichBrott.com

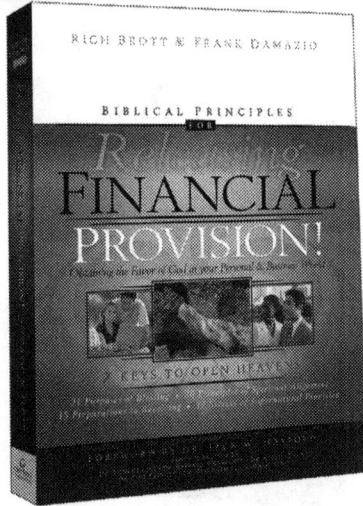

## Biblical Principles for Releasing Financial Provision!

*Obtaining the Favor of God in Your*
*Personal and Business World*

### By Rich Brott

7.5" x 10", 456 pages
ISBN 1-59383-021-1
ISBN (EAN) 978-1-59383-021-2

**abc**
Book Publishing

*Order online at:*
www.RichBrott.com
www.amazon.com
www.barnesandnoble.com
www.booksamillion.com
www.citychristianpublishing.com
www.bordersstores.com

## www.AbcBookPublishing.com

# Additional Resources *by Rich Brott*

## www.RichBrott.com

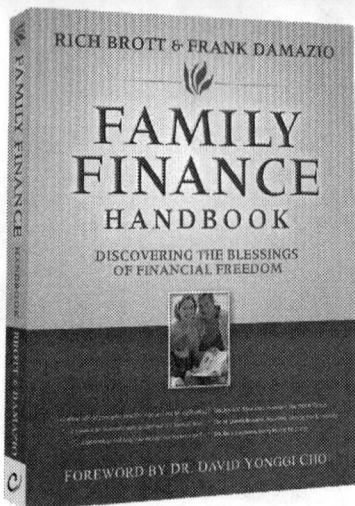

## Family Finance Handbook

*Discovering the Blessing*
*of Financial Freedom*

By Rich Brott & Frank Damazio

7.5" x 10", 288 pages
ISBN 1-914936-60-3
ISBN 978-1-914936-60-2

abc
Book Publishing

### Order online at:
www.RichBrott.com
www.amazon.com
www.barnesandnoble.com
www.booksamillion.com
www.citychristianpublishing.com
www.bordersstores.com

## www.AbcBookPublishing.com

# Additional Resources *by Rich Brott*

## www.RichBrott.com

## Also look for these new titles:

*A Biblical Perspective on Giving Generously*

*A Biblical Perspective on Tithing Faithfully*

*Achieving Financial Alignment*

*Activating Your Personal Faith to Receive*

*Successful Time Management*

**a**b**c**
Book Publishing

*Order online at:*
www.RichBrott.com
www.amazon.com
www.barnesandnoble.com
www.booksamillion.com
www.citychristianpublishing.com
www.bordersstores.com

## www.AbcBookPublishing.com

www.ingramcontent.com/pod-product-compliance
Lightning Source LLC
Chambersburg PA
CBHW060008100426

42740CB00010B/1434